Fear, Religion, Politics;

Well I'll Be Darned!!

By:

John E. Karlin, Ph.D.

With a Foreword by Melvyn G. Preisz, Ph.D.

White Owl Publishing
Oklahoma City, Oklahoma
Copyright 2018

Fear, Religion and Politics
Well, I'll Be Darned!

ISBN-978-0-692-16415-0

Manuscript prepared by, Gerry Lantagne

Published by White Owl Press
Oklahoma City, Oklahoma

Forward

This is not just a book, it is an epic statement of importance. This book is powerfully packed with truth. Just to read it is an affirmation of your belief in freedom. Just to read it is an act of protecting your freedoms. Just to read it is an exercise in the Founding Father's two requirements to maintain our freedoms: an "Enlightened Citizenry," and a commitment to "Eternal Vigilance."

It is noteworthy that Dr. Karlin has described so clearly the following severe dangers to our individual freedoms:

1) The inextricable link between the ultimate fear of death and religion.

2) The intertwining and linkage by the far religious right to politics, to the point of the "far religious right" being a racist political party, as much as it is a religion, whose ultimate goal is to turn the country into a "Theocracy."

3) The toxic intertwining and linkage of the "far religious right" with the most wealthy corporate corruption to dominate and take control of our government and our institutions at all levels, in order to turn the country into an "Oligarchy". All of them deny the value of truth, and they are formidable enemies of our Democracy.

I agree with Dr. Karlin's timely and insightful assessments of this unprecedented crisis. From my own psychological view point, these enemies of our individual freedoms have colluded to divide and conquer the good within us, and to continue to attack our personal consciousness from a buffet of lies.

Dr. Karlin suggests that by raising our personal awareness and enriching the level of our consciousness we can unite, re-affirm, defend our Constitution, and protect our freedom from the evil our malignant enemies represent. Freedom is not circumstantial. Freedom is a metaphysical state of being. Faith in our ability to enrich our consciousness of our free-dom, according to Dr. Karlin, is essential for its protection as is a re-commitment to our Founding Father's Constitution.

In conclusion, if you are not authentically conscious of the reality of freedom, as Dr. Karlin asserts, you may expe-rience a sense of liberty, but you are not free! To read and share this work is not just an act of citizenship, patriotism, true love of country and freedom, it is a revolutionary act from the hearts and minds of our Founding Fathers to date!

Respectfully,

Dr. Mel Preisz, Ph.D., LMFT.

Former Tenured Professor of Psychology and Chairman of the De-partment of Psychology at Oklahoma City University

Co-Owner of the Preisz-McMillin Clinic, Inc., Oklahoma City, Okla.

About the Author

Dr. John Karlin was born in Wellington, Kansas and graduated from Wellington Senior High School in 1965. He served in the Army as a Davy Crockett Crewman during the Viet Nam War. He received his undergraduate and master's degree from Wichita State University, Wichita, Kansas and his Ph.D. in Sociology from Louisiana State University, Baton Rouge, Louisiana. Dr. Karlin taught at the University level for over 20 years and last taught at Phillips University in Enid, Oklahoma. Upon retiring, he published '21st Century America A No Holds Barred View'. He currently lives in Tecumseh, Oklahoma and pursues numerous interests. Among recent professional activities, he made a formal paper presentation at the Eastern Sociological Society 2018 Annual Conference in Baltimore, Maryland. Previous recent formal presentations were at the Eastern Sociological Society 2016 Annual Conference in Boston, Massachusetts and the Pacific Sociological Association 2016 Annual Conference in Oakland, California. Dr. Karlin is a consultant for the Preisz-McMillin Clinic in Oklahoma City, Oklahoma.

Acknowledgements And Dedication

No well researched non-fiction book is produced without the help of numerous people. Special thanks to all the individuals who helped in the production of this book in many ways, from encouragement to the nuts and bolts of research and putting a book together. Those outstanding individuals and their primary contributions in alphabetical order are:

1. Gerry Lantagne; Resource and Computer work.
2. Judith Martin; Proof reading and Editing.
3. Dr. Mel Preisz; Consulting.
4. Rhonda Bell; Cover design and Art work.

All are greatly appreciated for their endless encouragement which was expressed in many ways. With their tremendous help, this book was produced and is dedicated to my parents and children; Merle and Evelyn (Zoglman) Karlin, John W., Rosalind and Nick Karlin.

John E. Karlin Ph.D.
karlinfirstnamejohn@yahoo.com

Table of Contents

Introduction

Page 1

Part One: *The Problem That Won't Go Away*

Page 3

Part Two: *The Dream*

Page 42

Part Three: *A Dream Gone Awry*

Page 81

References

Page 130

Introduction

The author considers himself a 'follower' of the philosophy of 'Jesus Christ of the gospels'. It does not matter whether the 'character' Jesus was even a real person or not. 'Jesus' the 'character' depicted in the gospels lived a certain life as described in those gospels. In that sense, no different than the 'character' depicted in the Epic of Gilgamesh. That life or 'character' reflects a philosophy of life. A philosophy expressed in what he (real or not) was depicted as doing and saying. One can identify or agree with that philosophy of life. It is a humanistic philosophy. One can consider him/herself a 'follower' simply by agreeing with and accepting it at least in most part as their own. The author finds no problem with the 'social gospel' of Jesus Christ, real or imaginary.

The 'Far Religious Right' in this work refers to three ultra-conservative groups; namely the Fundamentalists, Evangelicals, and Born-Again Christians. The three groups have more in common than differences. The things they have in common are more major and central to their belief systems. The differences are more minor variations, which are not as central to their belief systems. There are minor variations within each group. All three groups overlap to create what has come to be called the 'Far Religious Right.' This designation reflects the fact that they have become as much a political party or movement as they are a religion. Since some form of Fundamentalism is the most common and/or the most dominant aspect of all three, they are often referred to in this work just as 'Funda-

1

mentalists', or the 'Far Religious Right'. To refer to any one of the three is to refer to all three ('Dominionism Rising: A Theocratic Movement Hiding in Plain Sight', Frederick Clarkson).

This group comprises well over one-third of the Christian population of the United States. As a whole, they comprise the greatest threat and danger to religious freedom and liberty there is today. As a political force, they comprise the greatest threat and danger to Democracy and freedom today. At a minimum, they want freedom only for themselves and their religion, no one else. If given the power, they would imprison, torture, even kill others who were not just like them. Power can be unbelievably corrupting and in the hands of religious fanatics (like ISIS), it can be even more so. It can corrupt to the point of inhumanity and insanity. Freedom must be universal. It must be all inclusive. Where freedom does not exist for even one person, it exists for none because even the most horrific oppressor him/herself is not truly free. Scott Howard Phillips once observed: "You can't pick and choose which types of freedom you want to defend, you must defend all of it or be against all of it." The author of this work does not tread lightly, nicely or politely on those who oppose freedom. I give no apologies to those evil bastards.

The nature of the universe is such that things don't always work the way we would like. The author was told that maybe it would be best to approach the far religious right with understanding, care and love. After giving much thought to this, the author could only come up with the scenario of approaching a rabid dog with a tootsie roll.

Part One

The Problem That Won't Go Away

There are two facts of human life and existence. One is that humans are conscious of their own existence. Two is that they are mortal beings and some day they will die. The problem that death is inevitable will never go away. This has important implications and consequences for humans and the life they experience and lead. This is dealt with for example in three separate publications: Earnest Becker's classic work 'The Denial of Death', Sheldon Solomon et. al. 'The Worm at the Core: On the Role of Death and Life' and 'Death Anxiety and Religious Belief: An Existential Psychology of Religion' by Jonathan Jong and Jamin Halberstdadt. They deal with the basic psychological conflict that results from having a self-preservation instinct along with the realization that death is inevitable and generally unpredictable.

Death remains the largest threat, often terrifying, as well as the greatest challenge to humans. It is the single universal event that affects all of humanity in many more ways than we know or care to admit. According to **Symbolic Interaction Theory**, humans act toward things based, not on the thing itself, but on the basis of the meaning we put on it. Whatever meanings we attach to death has important consequences for our well-being. At the individual level, death attitudes matter; death defines personal meaning and determines how we live life. At the cultural, societal level, death also makes its universal presence in a broad range of social relations and functions, from family to religion to politics. How we relate to our own mortality is in turn mediated by the groups, society and culture with which we identify.

Over a century ago, William James called the knowledge that one must die "the worm at the core" of the human condition. Solomon et. al., argue the many ways the worm at the core guides our thoughts and actions, from the great art we create to the wars we wage. Building on Becker's classic work, they argue that fear of death powers almost everything we do, shining a light on the hidden motives that drive human beings and their behavior. They argue that the fear of death and the desire to transcend it, inspire us to buy expensive cars, crave fame and put our health at risk. They argue that the fear of death can prompt judges to levy harsher punishments, make children react negatively to people that are not like them and inflame intolerance and violence. They argue a need to divest ourselves of the cultural, social and personal illusions that keep us from accepting the inevitability of death.

All human activities and psychological inventions, creations, illusions and delusions are framed by death anxiety and colored by our group and individual efforts to resolve this inescapable and intractable existential reality ('Beyond Terror and Denial: The Positive Psychology of Death Acceptance', Paul T.P. Wong and Adrian Tomer). In his classic work, Becker argues that human civilization is ultimately an elaborate symbolic defense mechanism against the knowledge of our mortality which in turn, acts as the emotional and cognitive response to our basic survival mechanisms. A basic duality in human life exists between the physical world of objects and a symbolic world of human meanings. In 'The Social Construction of Reality', Berger and Luckman argue that: "human reality is a socially constructed reality." Society entails both objective and subjective realities in a dialectical process.

Since human life has a dualistic nature consisting of a physical body and a socially created symbolic 'self', or conception of 'self', we are able to transcend the dilemma of mortality through what Becker calls "heroism", by focusing our attention mainly on our symbolic self. This Symbolic self-focus takes the form of an individual's "immortality project", which is essentially a symbolic belief-system that ensures oneself is believed superior to physical reality. The attraction of religion in relation to this is the belief for Christians, in particular, that humans were created in the "image" of an all-powerful, superior being. By successfully living under the terms of the immortality project, people feel they can become heroic and thus part of something eternal, something that will never die as compared to their physical body.

The susceptibility of humanity to the lure of religious belief systems which says he/she has a 'soul' that cannot die, an "immortal" soul is strong. This in turn gives people the feeling that their lives have meaning, a purpose, and are significant in the grand scheme of the 'here-and-now'. Also, the future is assured in the religious lure of and promise of an "after-life". Being born in the "image" of an all-powerful superior being with an "immortal" soul destined for an eternal "after-life" of heavenly bliss makes humanity very vulnerable to even the most illogical and irrational of religious belief systems. These belief systems can even border on and cross the lines of sanity. They are out and out delusional. It explains why some have literally dropped their lives and went to some specified location on a very specific date (the end of the world) to wait for God to save them by picking them up in a space ship. Even the satirical church of the "flying spaghetti monster" wouldn't buy that one. How many "end times" have there been through history? Hundreds? Thousands? Maybe that is why they call them "end times", they never end.

The arbitrariness of human-invented immortality projects makes them, Becker argues, naturally prone to conflict. When one immortality project conflicts with another, it is essentially an accusation of living the wrong life, an evil life, that is perceived as a threat, and so sets the stage of conflict for both defensive and aggressive behavior. It is the foundation upon which behavior like Christians stoning each other to death for things like blasphemy are based. Each party will want to prove its belief system is superior, and thus they are superior, and it is the only acceptable way of life that will ensure the promise of an "after-life". It is in this way that immortality projects are the fundamental engine of human conflict such as genocide, wars, mass murders, bigotry and racism.

Conflict Theorists (in Sociology) would argue that overlaying this is the conflict over physical resources. Conflict generated by the private ownership of property. The fear of death and survival needs inflame conflict over the material resources needed to sustain life. Religion is the most prominent, universal and powerful "hero-system" because it not only provides an agreeable, absolute, black and white meaning to human life but also holds out the belief and promise of an "after-life" and an "immortal" soul. Religious "hero-systems" have produced conflicts since the dawn of humankind and will continue to do so as long as religion exists. This is why His Holiness the Dalai Lama argued in 'Beyond Religion Ethics for a Whole World' that: "Today, any religion-based answer to the problem of our neglect of inner values can never be universal, and so will be inadequate. What we need today is an ethics which makes no recourse to religion and can be equally acceptable to those with faith and those without; a secular ethics. The time has come to find a way of thinking about spirituality and ethics that is beyond religion."

Humankind must look to something else other than religion as the basis for relations between people. Extreme fear is produced by the mortality conflict. It in turn produces conflict between individuals and between groups. Humans try to manage this fear by embracing cultural values, paradigms, or symbolic systems that provide life with sustainable value and meaning. Cultural values, belief systems and symbols that help to manage the fear of death most commonly are those that offer literal immortality i.e. a belief in an "after-life", an "immortal" soul-religion. Because cultural and social values and belief systems determine what is meaningful, they also are the foundation for self-esteem and self-identity or "self", (who we perceive ourselves to be). For the individual, self-esteem provides a defense against the anxiety and fear produced by his/her own mortality.

Studies show that people who felt better about themselves also report having less death-related anxiety. People with strong self-esteem are less likely to be disabled by death anxiety. Self-esteem serves as a defense against anxiety. Society also serves this function. People derive protection against death anxiety from worldview faith as well as from their own self-esteem. Worldview faith is religious belief or some other conviction that human life is meaningful. All religions delineate, define and declare some meaning to life. It is through personal experience and social encounters that people learn what they should fear and not fear. Often, this is very irrational in that they fear the most that which is least likely to harm them, and fear the least, that which is most likely to harm them. Their fears are influenced by the interaction between cognitive development and social learning experiences. There have been many empirical studies of death anxiety, but important questions and issues also remain because of methodological limitations and the difficulties inherent in the subject. However, as a whole, the research points to some conclusions. Most people 'report' that they have a low to moderate level of death-related anxiety, especially men. Women report higher levels of death-related anxiety. People with mental and emotional disorders tend to have a higher level of death anxiety than the general population. It can be argued that irrational and illogical religious belief systems, in confrontation with reality, produce severe cognitive dissonance, which in turn takes its toll on the mental stability of the individual and produces emotional and psychological disorders. This may feed back into the dependence on religion as a denial mechanism and explain religious fanaticism. The greater the anxiety and panic, the greater the concern with being "saved".

The connection between death anxiety and gender is strong. In studies in which respondents are asked if they are anxious about death, one problem, similar to the 'denial of denial', is that both death anxiety and the denial of death involves the respondent's self-esteem and concept of self, that is, who they perceive themselves to be. People, especially men, may respond that they are not anxious about death because they do not want to admit that they are afraid, which would detract from or contradict their self-image of being a "man". This may explain why research has shown that women express more death anxiety than men. Also, women are raised to express their emotions while men are typically raised to suppress them. Men respond on the basis of their male image, of being strong, unafraid, "macho"; they are not supposed to be afraid of anything. It would not be 'manly' or masculine.

The 'denial of denial' involves thoughts, actions and behaviors which bolster confidence so that nothing needs to be changed in one's personal behavior. This form of denial overlaps with all of the other forms of denial, and it involves mostly self-deception. Self-esteem, self-concept clarity, existential well-being are functions of the interaction between self-reported levels of fear of death and death denial. Positive existential growth can come from individuals facing rather than denying their mortality ('Self-related Consequences of Death Fear and Death Denial', Philip Cozzolino). Not fearing and denying death can bolster important positive components of the self. Individuals low in death denial and death fear evidence an enhanced self that is valued, clearly conceived, and that has meaning and purpose.

Becker argues that the majority of human action, if not all, is taken to ignore, deny, or avoid the inevitability of death, the reality of one's own mortality. He states that the extreme terror of absolute annihilation and non-existence creates a very profound anxiety in people. It causes them to spend, if only subconsciously, their entire life trying to make sense of it and of life itself. Symbolic interactionists ('Symbolic Interactionism', Herbert Blumer) point to society's building of symbolic structures, cultures, meaning systems and religious belief systems through the symbolic interaction of it's members, to explain the significance of life, to delineate and define the good, the bad, and the ugly, to delineate and define (thus bringing into existence) good and evil. These meanings are then used to reward others who are "good" (usually people just like them) and to punish or kill those who are "bad". Those who are "bad" are usually those who do not hold to their cultural worldview and meanings.

Death anxiety is so intense that it generates most, if not all, of the specific fears and phobias people experience in everyday life. It is more tolerable, more compatible with one's self-image to transform that anxiety into numerous smaller distractions. No function of society or group to which one identifies with, is more crucial than it's strengthening of individual defenses against death anxiety. Many beliefs and practices are in the service of death denial, which reduces the experiencing of anxiety. Societal elements join with individual efforts to maintain the fiction that there is nothing to fear. Ritualistic behavior on the part of individuals, groups, and social institutions generally have the underlying purpose of channeling and finding use for what otherwise would surface as disorganizing, disruptive and chaotic death anxiety.

People are less 'in denial' when in safe circumstances and report having a low level of death anxiety. However, the anxiety surfaces when they are told of or perceive a threat. A threat may not be just in physical terms, the threat of bodily harm, but a threat to self-esteem and/or the belief system which allows the denial of death. This threat can be real or imaginary. Death anxiety is universal and is caused by thoughts of death. It is a feeling of fear and/or terror when one thinks of or contemplates the process of dying or non-existence. This is the terror of ceasing to 'be'. Predatory death anxiety dates back to earliest human who may be here today and eaten tomorrow. Death anxiety is so intense that it creates the irrational fear of the dead.

Death is the center of many traditions and organizations; customs relating to death are a feature of every culture around the world. Much of it revolves around the "afterlife". In society the nature of death and humanity's awareness of its own mortality, has for millennia been a concern of the world's religious traditions. This includes belief in resurrection or an afterlife with Abrahamic religions. Death is an important subject of religious doctrine. For example, death is seen in Judaism as tragic and intimidating because death puts a cessation to the possibility of fulfilling any commandments. There are a variety of beliefs about death and the afterlife within Judaism; for example, persons who come into contact with corpses are ritually impure.

Fear of the dead, a product of the fear of death, for example was salient in preliterate societies throughout the world. It is found in the parable of the Good Samaritan. The most basic and oldest form of death anxiety is fear of being injured or killed. Predatory anxiety can be stimulated by a variety of situations, including psychological and social, real or imagined. The most powerful form of death anxiety is existential death anxiety, which comes from the basic knowledge and reality that human life will end. Symbolic language and interaction has created the basis for existential death anxiety primarily through meanings constructed in communicative and behavioral interactions and exchanges.

Awareness of human mortality arose in the first human beings, and humans quickly developed a single basic defense through which they deal with the existential death anxiety it produced. That defense mechanism is denial in some form. Denial is constructed through a variety of mental mechanisms. The most universal and prominent of these mechanisms are religious belief systems. For modern humanity, the concept of self-esteem and 'self' or one's identity play a more major role. The most common use of denial is excessive and aggressive use of denial. Fear and denial is commonly the foundation of behaviors, like directing violence toward others, crime and deviance, violating social norms and boundaries, manic and sociopathic behaviors, neurotic and paranoid activities and religious rituals such as snake handlers and what has been called "holy rollers".

Most often, this use of denial is destructive, conflictual, and results in injury to self and others. It is as old as humankind. 'The Epic of Gilgamesh' is the oldest written story in the world ('Gilgamesh', Random House Webster's Unabridged Dictionary; 'The Epic of Gilgamesh; The Babylonian Epic Poem and Other

Texts in Akkadian and Sumerian' Trans. Andrew George). Written on 12 tablets in cuneiform script, it comes from ancient Sumerian literature. By 3,100 B.C., Sumerians had invented the earliest known writing by making wedge-shaped marks on clay tablets. As their writing evolved, the Sumerians used it to record not only economic exchanges, but also myths, prayers, and business contracts. It is a story about the adventures of the ruthless King of Uruk sometime between 2,750 and 2,500 B.C. Written in 2,150 to 1,400 B.C., it is the great Sumerian-Babylonian poetic work which predates Homer's Iliad by 1,500 years. It is the oldest piece of epic western literature, the oldest epic tale in the world which has important implications for the portrayal of man's struggle with his own mortality in literature.

'The Epic of Gilgamesh' is a story of the King of Uruk – Gilgamesh, and his adventures culminating in his abandonment of the denial of death. This epic story was discovered in the ruins of a library in Nineveh in 1853. This Akkadian version dates from around 1,300 to 1,000 B.C. It is an epic poem from ancient Mesopotamia. It is the earliest surviving great work of literature. The Epic is the literary history of Gilgamesh and begins with five Sumerian poems about Gilgamesh dating from the third dynasty of Ur. These independent stories were later used for the combined epic. The first surviving version of this combined epic dates to the 18th Century B.C. Written hundreds of years before the Bible, 'The Epic of Gilgamesh' is essentially the same story as much of the Bible.

Many themes, story elements, and characters in the Epic of Gilgamesh have very strong similarities in the Bible. For example, the accounts of the Garden of Eden. The similarities and parallels in the stories of Enkidu and Shamhat with the stories of Adam and Eve, have been well recognized by literary and biblical scholars. Another is that the flood in the Epic matches that of the Genesis flood so closely that it leaves no doubt that the Genesis account derives from the Epic. A final very specific example among others, is the very rare proverb about the strength of a triple-stranded rope. In both books, word for word, is: "a triple-stranded rope is not easily broken". The whole issue of the meaning of life and the fear of death in the Epic of Gilgamesh is incorporated also into the Bible.

In the Epic of Gilgamesh, Enkidu challenges Gilgamesh to a test of strength. Gilgamesh wins and the two become close friends. However, Gilgamesh and his friend Enkidu anger the Gods. The Gods decide to punish Gilgamesh with the death of Enkidu. Gilgamesh falls into a deep grief and recognizes his own mortality through the death of his friend. He questions the meaning of life and the value of human accomplishment in the face of ultimate annihilation. The emotional distress about Enkidu's death causes Gilgamesh to undertake a long and perilous journey to discover the secret of eternal life. Throwing aside all of his pride and vanity, Gilgamesh sets out to find the meaning of life and finally some way of defeating death. He thus connects the meaning of life to death.

The grief of Gilgamesh and the questions his friend's death invoke resonate with every human being who has wrestled with the meaning of life in the face of death. It is a major theme in the Bible and continues to be a major theme in religion today. Gilgamesh searches for immortality as he deeply mourns Enkidu's death and worries about his own mortality. Today, in religion, the answer to immortality, the denial of death, is the belief in an "after-life", and all that it will bring embellished with the phantasies of "heavenly bliss" for the "righteous". But Gilgamesh learns a different lesson. Gilgamesh searches for Utnapishti, an immortal man who survived the great flood, a precursor to the biblical Noah. Gilgamesh finally finds Utanapishti who tells Gilgamesh "to go without sleep for a week. Gilgamesh fails the test and realizes in despair that if he cannot beat sleep he has no hope of conquering death." ('The Epic', Andrew George).

Gilgamesh is told to accept his mortality, as he cannot change it. He is told that; "life, which you look for, you will never find for when the gods created man, they let death be his share, and life withheld in their own hands." ('The Alternative Tradition', James Thrower, "Chapter VII: Mesopotamia', Henri Frankfort). He learns that life and death are connected. That the meaning of death can only be found in the meaning and living of life and thus, immortality can only be embedded in the meaning of life, not in the denial of death. Previously a harsh and cruel ruler, Gilgamesh realizing this then returns to Uruk, and becomes a good King. The Epic of Gilgamesh and the Bible show what Becker states in 'The Denial of Death'; "the idea of death, the fear of it, haunts the human animal like nothing else, it is a mainspring of human activity, activity designed largely to avoid the fatality of death, to overcome it by denying in some way, that it is the final destiny for man."

Nothing can evoke more emotion than the fear of death unless it is deep, extreme, fanatical, religious belief. In fact, to the degree that crime is an emotional act, religion is one of the most common variables across the board from perversion and assaults to child molestation and mass murders. Becker argues that humans are able to grasp the inevitability of death, that death creates an anxiety in humans, and it strikes at unexpected times and random moments. Thus, it's nature is essentially unknowable and largely unpredictable. This causes great insecurity. It causes people to spend their time, energy, material and cognitive resources to understand, explain, forestall and avoid or prevent it.

It has created much myth and folklore of the "fountain of youth" genre since early humankind. From the beginning the fear of death was not only itself powerful, but it created dramatic responses to it, if only psychological in nature.

Can religion even exist without the denial of death i.e. a belief in an after-life or immortal soul? Imagine a religion totally devoid of any concept what-so-ever of any kind, of an after-life, no heaven, no hell, no reincarnation, etc., nothing. One can argue that the fear of death even created God. If there was no such thing as an after-life, then there would be no point, no purpose at all in believing in a God. God, it can be argued was created in conjunction with the belief in an after-life to bolster this belief in an after-life and thus, the denial of death. In the earliest humans, fear of death came before the belief in a God. How did 'God' come to be 'experienced' and, thus 'believed' to be something 'out-there'? Durkheim in his classical work 'The Elementary Forms of Religious Life', argued that 'God' is the deification of the reification of society. When people worship 'God', what they are actually worshipping is their own society experienced and then projected as something real and as being 'out-there'.

Durkheim points out that this is why throughout the history of humankind, different cultures, societies, have produced different 'gods', each one a reflection of itself i.e. society. In 'The Elementary Forms of Religious Life', Durkheim's purpose was to identify the social origin and function of religion. Durkheim focused on the 'sacred' and argued that it is at the very core of a religion. Sacred things were simply the tribe's ideals that the tribe fixed on material objects. They are only collective forces hypostasized, moral forces; they are made up of the 'spectacle' of society itself and not of sensations coming only from the physical world. Thus, Durkheim argues that humans experience 'society' as a 'spectacle'. He argues that religion emerged in the early hunter-gatherer tribes as group emotions ran higher and higher in growing larger and larger collectives. This gave them a sense of some hidden force (the emotions, especially when acted out of the group as a whole) driving them.

Over time, emotions become symbolized and interactions amidst the group ritualized, religion develops, giving rise to the sacred. Durkheim saw this in the most ancient religion, totemism which expresses the essential elements of religion. Religion has its origins in totemism. He argues that society is the soul of religion, that society itself is the foundation of all religious belief. Totems are collective symbols that represent both the tribe which is projected outwardly because it is experienced as something or a powerful force 'out-there', and thus, the totem also represents 'God'. The primary purpose of religion is to allow people to imagine their own society, express its social unity, it's collective thought, collective emotions and collective experiences and sharing of them. Totemism is an early expression of this primary purpose. It is the basis of all religious thought.

Durkheim argues totemism is symbolic: "the totem is a symbol, a material expression of something else. It is a symbol of society and God; there-fore, God and society are one and the same. if the totem is both the symbol of society and of God, are these not the same? The God of the clan must there-fore be the clan itself but transformed and imagined in the physical form of the plant or animal species that serves as totems." Once God is brought into existence in this way, it remains and is maintained in tradition, folklore, customs and rituals. The totem, for example, comes to be replaced by a cross. Durkheim also focused on the rituals and ceremonies of primitive totemic tribes. The deification of the reification of society is grasped in those rituals and ceremonies.

In one ceremony, the tribe would build very large bonfires, which they would wildly dance around twenty-four hours a day for many days and nights. They also built dirt mounds upon which they would place items that they wanted to become sacred. The individual was submerged and engulfed in this frenzy of wild dancing and shouting people twenty-four hours a day for days and nights, until the point of utter exhaustion and collapse. Giant fires, sparks and smoke engulfed the whole scene. The individual could not help but to experience with extreme intensity, to his very being, all this forceful, dynamic impinging upon him from out side of him, from 'out-there'. At the point of collapse the individual would then go to his mound of dirt, slash his penis with a knife and bleed on the items he had placed there to make them 'sacred'.

Durkheim questioned, if you took one of these individuals aside and asked, "what are you doing? You just about cut your penis off with a knife" How could that person answer? What could he possibly say that would make any sense at all? The answer was, "I did not do that, 'mana' made me do it. I was possessed by "mana". "Mana," of course, was this very powerful force that the person felt, to his very being' had possessed him and made him do it. The individual made the items sacred by bleeding on them. By transferring his blood and, thus transferring "mana," of which he was possessed, to the items, he made them sacred. Durkheim asked what was really there in the physical world? What was this individual actually experiencing? The answer presented itself. He was experiencing his own society in all its 'spectacle', the intensity and excitement of the ceremony itself. He experienced 'mana' out there as a powerful force. Thus, humankind reified his own society as being 'out-there,' then deified it into a God, "Mana."

Humans alone recognize that death is unavoidable, and there is an overwhelming psychological impetus to overcome this inevitable tragedy. The role of the 'sacred' in this endeavor is as a defense and a denial. Across human history and cultures, violence is universally (as is the denial of death) claimed by the perpetrators to be a sublime matter of moral virtue. Without virtue, it is very difficult to kill large numbers of people (as in invasions and conquests) that are innocent of direct harm to others. Violence is often carried out with a conviction of moral righteousness. Violent acts are undertaken in the name of sacred objects. The sacred object is a transcendental idea or ideal or entity like a totem, that holds the group together. Violent acts are undertaken as virtue, anything and everything for the sake of sacred objects.

When violence is undertaken in defense of the sacred, then violence for the sake of a transcendental moral conception, transcendent objects, in the name of which humans then are willing to fight, kill or die are interchangeable. Wars are often engaged in to prove whose God or 'Sacred' object was supreme. Wars were engaged in, in the name of and under the vindictive gaze of powerful divinities, Gods or Kings. Why rulers called for war and why individuals would volunteer in response to the call were one and the same, i.e. in the name of the 'sacred.' We may be inhumane and barbaric in deed and act, but if we rescue, protect, and defend God's land (sacred) etc., we have performed the greatest deed in the world ('Talking to the Enemy: Violent Extremism, Sacred Values, and What It Means to Be Human', Scott Atran).

The fear of death creates anxiety, which produces society, that in turn begets religion, all of which go into creating who you are. This is why religion is based on and thrives off of fear. Religion was one of earliest humanity's tools of social control. Control of people was enhanced through fear. Religion was and is a tool of social control. The fear of death is at the core, and it is the foundation of this continuum. Symbolic Interactionists argue that through symbolic communication (language being the ultimate symbolic system) humans simultaneously create, maintain and/or change in an ongoing process, themselves, each other, and society. The existence of self 'in' society and the deification of the reification of society is the foundation for the belief that each human is 'born' in the 'image' of 'God'. As expressed by Martin Heidegger in 'Being and Time,' our everyday existence is characterized by complete immersion in the ways of the world, culture and society. Culture and society fascinate us and our lives are completely caught up in its rhythms, activities and spectacle. It is being in the world as a whole. The human being finds him/herself in a world that is richly meaningful and fascinating. The world is homely, even cozy.

Heidegger took note of the strong tendency of humans to exist as 'das man', "the one" or "the they". Das man represents the anonymous or average member of the social group, and thus the modes of thought, belief and behavior which are considered normal and expected. Our strong tendency to think, behave, and live "as one does." ('History of the Concept of Time', Martin Heidegger). Once internalized as 'self', we take the values of our society for granted and immerse ourselves in social roles and societal games. We

19

"do what one does" without question. It is a deep-rooted need to conform. Likewise, Becker argues that people spend their lives creating, living and believing in cultural and societal elements that give their lives significance and meaning. Fear causes the succumbing to an extreme identification with society. Most people find it much safer and easier to lose themselves in the crowd and thus feel more secure. "What we call worldliness simply consists of such people who, if one may so express it pawn themselves to the world." ('The Sickness unto Death', Soren Kierkegaard).

Heidegger argued that fear is always fear of something threatening, some particular thing in the world; fear always has an object; i.e. like fundamentalists' fear of homosexuality or fear of science. Fear is fearful of something particular and determinant ('What is a Thing', Heidegger). Fear is rarely if ever, logical or rational. A gun is a denial of fear. There is no logic in worshipping a deity that demands that you live in perpetual fear. Heidegger recognizes that anxiety is also a mood that is powerful in the Christian tradition, that the self's conversion is undergone in relation to the fear of death and death itself. Generally, we do not face up to our own mortality, but instead we evade it in a myriad of ways. We tell ourselves that death is not relevant to the living and that to think about it is morbid and a waste of time, or we relate to death impersonally.

To reiterate, Becker argues that people spend their lives creating and believing in cultural and social elements that give their lives significance and meaning. Cultural and societal values, beliefs, and life styles that allow them to stand out as individuals, even in their conformity to them. For Becker, fear of death is the primary motivation in human behavior in doing this and relates it to the concept of self-esteem as 'heroism': "the problem of heroics is the central one of human life, that it goes deeper into human nature than anything else, because it is based on organismic narcissism and on the child's need for self-esteem and the condition for his life" (it is a security blanket). Society itself is a codified hero system, which means that society itself is everywhere a living myth of the significance of human life, a defiant creation of meaning. The greatest myth is that of the immortality embedded in religion's "after-life" and "immortal" soul.

Heidegger emphasized the impact that the threat of death has because it is conclusively determined, that it is inevitable for every human being, and it unmasks it's indeterminant nature via the truth that usually one never knows when or how death is going to come. He argues that all human existence is embedded in time; the past, present, future, and when contemplating the future, people confront the notion of death. He argues then that this creates a great anxiety. Mortality salience, the awareness by an individual that his death is inevitable, causes existential anxiety that may be lessened by the individual's sense of self-esteem as derived from the individual's cultural worldview. When humans contemplate their mortality and vulnerability to death, they direct their actions to either avoiding death or distracting themselves from realizing it's reality. Almost all human activity is driven by the fear of death, as in the case of reproduction.

Mortality salience entails the conflict that humans have to face both their instinct to survive, to avoid death completely, and their knowledge that avoiding death is ultimately futile. Religious individuals, especially fundamentalists, being more rigid, inflexible, and authoritatively oriented in their strict religious beliefs, are less vulnerable to mortality salience manipulations and so religious believers engage in other worldview defenses to a lesser extent than non-religious individuals. It locks them into an isolated single worldview. Since one's cultural worldview or one's self-esteem, serves a death defying function, then threatening these constructs produces defenses aimed at restoring psychological 'immortality,' that is, returning the individual to a feeling of invulnerability.

Any threats real or imagined are experiential reminders of

21

one's own mortality. They can produce highly irrational and illogical defenses that extend to all areas of life, for example, Fundamentalism is a religion of denialism. It believes in "creationism." Evolution directly contradicts creationism, which in turn detracts from religion's denial of death. Evolution is thus a denial of the denial of death which terrorizes, horrifies and frightens the far religious right. Evolution is an undisputed fact within the scientific community and in academia, where the level of support for evolution is universal; it is based on irrefutable facts.

Yet, the far religious right, sometimes referred to as flat earthers, completely rejects evolution based on nothing but scriptures over 2,700 years old written by people who 'knew' that the world was flat and magical thinking. The percentage of science denying "flat earthers" has been increasing, so much so that Neil de Grasse Tyson felt compelled to comment: "For me, the fact that there's a rise of flat earthers (people who actually believe the earth is flat) is evidence of two things. One, we live in a country that protects free speech, and, two, we live in a country with a failed educational system." It is not that education has failed, but that education and science, is being rejected by more and more fundamentalists.

Theirs is an ideological-theocratic position which reacts by refusing reality and truth as based on concrete objective fact. They engage in denialism to protect a fantasy which is critical to their identity. Legitimate dialogue is not a valid option for them because they are only interested in and committed to protecting bigoted, irrational, illogical, unreasonable ideas from scientific facts. For fundamentalists, the facts are unacceptable because they have none. It is group denialism, struggling with the trauma of change; they turn away from reality in favor of a more comfortable lie, a more comfortable fantasy ('Fantasyland How America Went Haywire', Kurt Andersen). Any threat to the worldview of the far religious right produces derogation of and negative aggressive behavior toward all others that are not just like them.

This reaction is much stronger than any other religious group.

Greenberg et. al. had Christian students evaluate other Christian and Jewish students that were similar demographically but differed in their religious affiliation. After being reminded of their ultimate death, Christian participants evaluated fellow Christians more positively, and Jewish participants more negatively. Thus, bolstering self-esteem in mortality salience situations leads to less worldview defense and more derogation of dissimilar others. Denialism is pervasive in the far religious right's world view. It covers literally every reality from evolution to all others who are not a carbon copy of themselves (Greenberg et. al., 'Evidence for terror management theory. II: The effects of mortality salience on reactions to those who threaten or bolster the cultural worldview', Journal of Personality and Social Psychology, 58 (2), 1990., 'Terror management theory of self-esteem and cultural worldviews: Empirical assessments and conceptual refinements', Advances in Experimental Social Psychology. 29 (S 61), 1997).

Belief in the after-life is a powerful tool of denial of mortality. Problematically, it becomes inextricably intertwined with one's self-esteem and concept of self or identity and the identity of the group to with which one identifies. This fosters tribalism and a tribal mentality. The hope for immortality is one of the principle motivations for religious beliefs. Empirical research confirms this proposition. Psychological studies show that heightened awareness of one's vulnerability to death intensifies belief in supernatural agents. The roots of the human longing for an afterlife go back to earliest humankind, certainly as recorded in the Epic of Gilgamesh. Humankind is plagued with an existential fear about death and other forms of irretrievable loss and injury, such as permanent disability. This fear, terror, is triggered not only by concern over events that may affect one directly but also may fall on loved ones or even the tribe.

Fear is anticipatory, and despair is the response to loss already experienced; it is a state of mind of those overcome by loss. Those who are religiously inclined and terrified of their own impending death or that of a loved one, or a friend, will not shed the security of an after-life. In times of crisis, in particular, the strongest source of denial is religiously based hopes. The allure of such hopes to those who are already religious or have religious inclinations, in times of crisis are overpowering. There is no chance that those who are religious will reject religious 'solutions' when they are experiencing fear or despair. They are not particularly susceptible to rational thinking or logic. They do not realize that immortality, regardless of how perceived, is an illusion and provides at best, only the thin vail of a false hope.

One cannot begin to develop a mature, rational perspective on life until all illusions relating to the supernatural are stripped away and recognized as a method of escapism and the denial of reality. The far religious right is tribal, illogical, irrational and has become as much a political party as it is a religion. It is a political movement that threatens freedom and liberty. In discussing the religious right, Blow ('Moore, Trump and the Right's New Religion') states that: "all the pretense of any "moral" majority and "moral" authority has vanished into the very impulses that fed it. Tribal, racial-ethnic anxiety, panic and hostility, patriarchy and sexism, piety now is postscript. The motivation now is anger (tribal), fear of cultural displacement, and anxiety about the erosion of (white) privilege and the guarantees it once provided, from physical safety to financial security. Tribal fear is dominant; practically anything and everything is capable of eliciting the innate, primitive fear from within, even when there is no rational basis for it.

Why would one "fear" the law of another country if one doesn't live there? As Blow states: "their driving motivation was to make religious law into American law, really not so unlike the Sharia law they so fear and despise." Fundamentalist religion is literally an ideology, philosophy of tribal fear, with fear of death being transformed into fear of God and hell. There is no logic

24

in worshipping a deity that demands that you live in perpetual fear. Tribal fear is literally taught along with beliefs about God and the after-life i.e. heaven and hell. In fact, fear is so central to religion (not just Fundamentalism), it is a necessity for the survival of religion. This is why fear must be perpetuated in even the earliest years. To do this, fundamentalists support private school vouchers and home schooling rather than public schools where students are taught to think for themselves.

Evangelical founder of Focus on the Family, James Dobson has proclaimed that: "those who control what young people are taught, and what they experience, what they see, hear, think, and believe, will determine the future course for the nation" ('Children at Risk', James C. Dobson). This statement shows not just an emphasis on indoctrination, but mind control. Fundamentalists typically home school their children, usually with no outside input, or they put them in far-right ultra-conservative Christian schools. This is an effort to isolate them or cut them off from learning what would open doors to critical thought, about which they are in fear, horror and terror. Mind control is the key concept in fundamentalist education. Dobson states: "Our spiritual should begin before children can even comprehend what it is all about."

What Dobson advocates and wants is not just indoctrination but out and out brainwashing. The priority in what is taught is not just biblical verses and prayers but the teaching of fear itself. As Dobson states: "I firmly believe in acquainting children with God's judgment and wrath while they are young, the wages of sin is death, and children have the right to understand that fact." This exposes the desire, intent, to teach fear itself. Fundamentalists believe that children need to learn discipline and obedience through fear as based on Proverb 22.15. "A major function of fundamentalist religion is to bolster deeply insecure and fearful people." ('Rescuing the Bible from Fundamentalism', Bishop John Spong). Fear, anxiety, insecurity, put never ending pressure on Christians to "convince themselves" that they have been "saved", that "they" are going to heaven even if no one else is. Indeed, part of convincing themselves "they" are going to heaven requires the belief that others ("them") are not.

Fundamentalist men expect unquestioning, automatic obedience, motivated by fear, whether they are children or women. They are autocratic, patriarchal and dictatorial in their relations with females ('Characteristics of the Incestuous Family', Jackie J. Hudson). One of the most common variables correlated with child and spouse abuse is fundamentalist religion. Theirs is a triple fear. The innate fear of death, fear of the wrath of God and hell and tribal fear, fear generated by the beliefs and perceptions of the group. These triple aspects of fear when in combination invariably generate pathological horror and terror. Fear is taught and learned through harsh discipline and punishment even for very minor infractions like simply not paying attention. As stated by Irwin Hyman of the National Center for the Study of Corporal Punishment and Alternatives; "it is increasing (corporal punishment) in the Christian Academies with a fundamentalist bent."

This is significant in light of the fact that much of it already constitutes child abuse (Spanking on the decline in U.S. Schools', USA Today, 1996). American Christians have three different 'Gods' which can serve to separate American Christians into three groups. The largest group, well over one-third of American Christians are the fundamentalists or far religious right. Their 'God' is the vengeful, vindictive, punishing God of the old testament. They almost exclusively support, campaign for and vote for "Get tough on Crime" politicians and support the death penalty as if it were one of the ten commandments. The next group, less than a third of American Christians are those whose 'God' is the "loving" God of the new testament. The smallest group's 'God' is the God that is amenable to and compatible with science and progress.

The human mind is a two-edged sword. It can both benefit and kill us with fear. The mind that can imagine a useful tool can also imagine spiritual kingdoms, invent a 'divine' creation, terror of a hell, engage in magical thinking, tribalism, and demonization that creates a disconnect with reality. In this primal function, the human imagines itself in the image of a God. Clinging to our 'divine' prerogatives, we cannot avoid that in our fantasies of godlike superiority are the seeds of neurosis, paranoia and sociopathology. The imagination proceeds to invent sinister hells, sumptuous heavens, and imaginary Gods. Religion is among the least grounded in reality belief systems invented by humankind, especially Fundamentalism.

Only a naturalistic perspective on life and death is grounded in reality. The natural world cannot wish away the finality of death or other irretrievable losses. It cannot provide acceptable answers to those who demand wish fulfillment and rely on magical thinking, but it well establishes the understanding that religion and belief in immortality are illusions. We can resist the temptation and lure of wishful thinking in times of crisis which only makes things worse, by focusing on the reality that nature and all its processes are awesome, understandable, real, and we are part of it. With our focus firmly fixed on the facts of nature and reality, we can truly appreciate not only what life can and cannot offer, but what the role of life and death is all about.

If we cannot make that adjustment to external reality of which we are a part, we fall prey to anxiety and fear, a straitjacket of irrationality that restricts our ability to make reasonable choices. Then the unreal becomes our reality, and we flounder in the terrors of our own imagination. Death is simply a natural part of a natural process. We begin dying the minute we are born; this is the process called 'aging'. It is part of the entropy of the universe, we are all dying creatures, a tiny blimp in history, a cosmic belch in eternity. Our lives flash by from birth to death like a beam of light. It has the career of a mosquito. The psychology of life includes death. Death a random event, an accident as perceived by other animals, is unnecessarily made a tragedy by our minds, and tragedy begs for a reason. The mind readily provides pre-constructed reasons from our culture. Some are make-believe, some are wishful thinking, and others are the psycho-babble of theologian's magical thinking. Logic, rationality, and science gives us the opportunity of basing our decisions and ethical choices on factual data. True relationships with each other and nature of which we are a part, need to be based on fact, rather than on fantasy, superstitions and ignorance. Religion was created through the magical thinking of pre-science flat-earthers as a means for humans to cope with their own mortality. Beliefs in life after death reduce the effects of mortality salience on worldview defenses. Primitive humans used their cognitive abilities to solve practical problems of survival and everyday life.

As their cognitive abilities developed, so did their explicit awareness of death emerge early in the process. Once this awareness materialized and death became a haunting reality, the fear and terror of it created and put pressure on emerging and changing conceptions of reality. Any belief system that was to be widely accepted by the group and provide cohesiveness to the group had to also create a means of managing this terror and fear. Primitive humans may have begun burying their dead for purely practical reasons, like avoiding diseases, etc., but eventually these practices went from primarily the practical to primarily the symbolic. They became ritualistic. They became largely if not wholly performed and enacted as symbolic ritual performances reflecting the supernatural belief systems of the group or tribe.

The most obvious was the placing of food and other necessities of life within the grave or burial chamber. This was a product of a belief system that included life after death. Religion is the most universal, common and predominant of these belief systems. Research on the subject suggests that the more religious one is, the less anxious one is about death because the individual may associate death with another beginning. This life after death, is promised and embellished by most religions. This is universal and provides evidence that religion was created as a means for humans to cope with their own mortality. Thus, to attack an individual's religion, is to attack not only his self-esteem and identity but his ability to deny death. This can and has produced extreme violence even mass murder and genocide toward others who are not of one's faith, especially among fundamentalist religious belief systems like ISIS.

The thought of death causes a different degree of anxiety for different individuals depending on many factors and situations. Religious beliefs provide a symbolic denial of death which may be weak in the face of immanent assured death. It also depends on the degree of 'religiosity' or depth of the belief. The higher the degree of religiosity and involvement, and the more depth of the belief and intensity, the stronger the symbolic denial. These religious belief systems can also provide an impetus and support for extreme violence toward others. They can provide a buffer to feelings of guilt or shame in the killing of another by way of magical thinking. When killing another, one can feel solace in the notion that the person who is killed will actually live on in perhaps even a better afterlife. "Send them to their maker."

This psychological mechanism is not anywhere near as prominent as the killing of others, especially those not of your faith, tribe, because they threaten your beliefs in the afterlife and thus your ability to deny the inevitability of death. This is one reason why it is relatively easier for religious leaders, in many cases, to lead their followers into acts of violence, war and genocide, more so than other leaders. This is one reason that the U.S. was founded on the principles of secular idealism and both freedom of and freedom from religion. Many citizens have strong beliefs about the role of religion, Christianity in particular, as the basis of morality. Many Christians reject the founding father's insistence on religious freedom and liberty and the doctrine of separation of church and state.

The far religious right's God is a vengeful, vindictive, punishing

God who watches over our shoulder every minute of every day with wrath and punishment in hand. They are strong believers in religious retribution. The attitude of religious retribution views social problems and maladies as a sign that God has punished humans for their sins. This view includes just about anything and everything emanating from humanity and society, as well as even nature as in natural disasters. They are very focused on violations of their ideas of common morality real or imagined. It is similar to religious retribution, the idea that social problems etc., are the result of a violation of some perceived common morality. They are absolutists when it comes to conceptions of morality. For example, the kids cartoon character 'sponge bob square pants' is seen as immoral and a sinner because 'sponge bob' (not even a real person) is gay and promotes homosexuality in their worldview.

They perceive the morals of society as objective facts. For them, there is something obvious within each deviant or sinful act, belief or condition that makes it different from religious morality ('Social Deviance', Tim Delany). Religious violence has been one of the most common characteristics of humanity throughout history. Religious leaders tend to be charismatic figures in close affinity with the emotions of their followers. Research has shown that compared to other types of leaders, the charismatic leader is much more favored by religious followers and religious leaders tend to be charismatic leaders. The most effective types of these leaders are ones who convince their followers that their violence toward others is just, righteous, ordained by God and in defense of God himself. This was the secret of Joan of Arc's phenomenal success. She convinced the French soldiers that they were not fighting for her or even for France but that they were fighting for God.

In 'The Battle for God', Karen Armstrong discusses the far religious right as a product of anxiety, fear and rage. Fundamentalism "represents a widespread disappointment, alienation, anxiety, and rage that no government can safely ignore." And "fundamentalists see conspiracy everywhere and are sometimes possessed by a rage that seems demonic." Armstrong argues that it is fundamentalist fears that produce fundamentalist theologies, beliefs, and ideologies. To fundamentalists, the world around them and everyday life "seems godless", drained of meaning, and even "satanic." Their paranoid thoughts of vengeance "would undoubtedly be diagnosed as a disturbance." The "depth of this neurosis" produces exclusion, hatred and violence, indeed, they become sociopathic.

Fundamentalist's whole worldview, their reality, is a product of anxieties and fears; they are a textbook case for disturbances in the Diagnostic and Statistical Manual (DSM). Again, as Bishop John Spong put it: "A major function of fundamentalist religion is to bolster deeply insecure and fearful people." Michael Franklin and Marian Hetherly argue that fundamentalist "evil imagination", which includes diverse forms of hostility, hatred, and violence, is a response to the anxiety and fear associated with powerlessness, and absolute dependence on Faith ('How Fundamentalism Affects Society', The Humanist). Fundamentalism creates conflicts some of which, are aggressive, violent and long lived. Conflict is often driven by unfulfilled needs and the fears related to those needs. The most common fear in intractable conflict is the fear of losing one's identity and/or security.

Fear can cause extreme and irrational behavior in people. Mattil states: "The common thread that weaves violent political movements together is fear – it is always there. Whenever we ask why people hate, or why they are willing to kill or die for a cause, the answer is invariably fear." ('What in the Name of God?: Fundamentalism, Fear & Terrorism', James F. Mattil). It was an observation issued by President Franklin Roosevelt in his first inaugural address in 1933: "We have nothing to fear but fear itself." Fear is a very personal and powerful emotion, people are social in nature, with shared values, religion, tradition, language, etc. Whenever the basic characteristics that bond a group together and give them cohesiveness are threatened,

31

the group will also attempt to get rid of the threat, often times through violent means. The Christians of Colonial America were out and out barbaric in their treatment of native Americans.

Oftentimes leaders use fear to their political advantage. Leaders need support from those they lead and, one way to gain this support is by playing on the fears of the people. Leaders even intentionally deepen these fears for their own purposes. The most powerful fear to control the fearful is fear that plays on people's emotions; it is an irrational fear fabricated on and intensified by ignorance. Since public support is essential for political leaders, they can gain this support by addressing, playing off of, and/or causing the fears of their supporters. Leaders can use fear especially irrational fear which never questions itself, as a motivational tool. People controlled by their own irrational fears never question why they fear or the leader playing on it. This is the fear produced by religion. They are "believers" not "thinkers".

Many experts and analysts refer to fundamentalism as more dangerous and more obtuse than the more traditional terrorism associated with separatist and nationalist movements. There are surprising similarities between Islamic, Christian and Jewish fundamentalists far beyond any similarity from all three being religions of Abraham. Religious fundamentalists often share some common traits and motivations with secular dissidents engaged in political violence. Religious fundamentalists are united by fear. Fear is the common denominator. They fear change, and loss of influence. They especially fear the effects of modernization, science and education, if it undermines the teachings of their religion. They fear a future they can't control, understand, or even comprehend.

These fears are common among fundamentalist Christians of every stripe. We are all told about moral decay, decadence, and the influence of the irreverent. These are the evils of which religious teaching warns. It is teaching to insure exclusion and isolation. These fears resonate loudest with people frustrated with the outside world, frustrated by political and economic systems they can neither understand or control. They can not even understand themselves. Extremely tribal, they huddle together mumbling and grunting to each other like a primitive tribe who has just seen a stranger from another land that they have never seen before. Religion holds for them meaning and offers hope, or at least future salvation. It offers simple, black and white, easy to understand answers based on the scriptures and magical thinking. If something bad happens, that is Satan's work. If something good happens, thank God. Typically, they are people who are older, rural, mired in poverty and have the least. They lack hope and education. Fear also connects the myriad of nationalist, separatist, white supremacists and other groups, all overlapping, who also engage in political violence.

Fear is an essential underlying motivator for and leads to violence and terrorism. People are social beings, gregarious animals, who come together in groups with shared values, religion, culture, language, tradition, heritage, or location in a common hope for survival and prosperity. Whenever the core characteristics that bond a group together comes under threat, the group will attempt to change the situation that poses the threat or, failing that, they will attempt to repeal the threat and strengthen their group cohesiveness. Leaders realizing this exploit popular fears for personal advantage by exaggerating the threats to the group. Nothing acts upon people more than the urgency and motivational power of fear. The problem of mortality will never go away. Maybe someday if we abandon the denial of death like Gilgamesh, the problems engendered by trying to deny it will.

Ironically, when one uses religion to escape the fear of death and one's own mortality, psychologically their actions are the equivalent of jumping out of the frying pan into the fire. In Christianity in particular the 'afterlife' is characterized as having two dramatically different possibilities. According to Christian doctrine, one will either go to 'heaven' or one will go to 'hell'. 'Heaven' is embellished with such fantastic pleasures that it stretches the imagination beyond limits to even try to comprehend or envision it. This, while just the word 'hell' alone elicits sheer terror, the most terrifying word in the realm of language and horror, is hell! This is the fire! How does one know or convince himself that he is going to 'heaven' and not 'hell'?

Not knowing creates as much if not more anxiety, fear and terror as the reality of mortality! The Christian true believer has simply replaced one problem or source of fear with another. It could be argued that the Christian is now even more anxious, fearful, and terrified to the degree that he still struggles with the original fear of death but now also struggles with the anxiety, fear and terror of going to hell rather than heaven. Arguably, the harshest of Christian doctrines was 17th Century Calvinist doctrine, specifically, the doctrine of 'pre-destination'. This is the belief that before one was even born, that God had already decided that they were going to either heaven or hell and that there was absolutely nothing that they could do to change that destiny. Martin Luther also championed the notion of 'predestination'. To the true believer this had to be a devastating thought, one that could drive one to madness. How does one convince him/herself (escape the terror) that he was 'chosen' (before birth) to go to heaven and not hell? Anxiety, fear, sheer terror! Calvin himself had no problem with this as he 'knew' he was a 'chosen' one.

Calvin did however, provide a psychological 'out' for the true believer. The kind of psychological 'out' or mechanism to escape mortality or, in the case of the afterlife dilemma i.e. heaven or hell, can have different consequences and conflicts for true believers and all others. For example, fundamentalism by it's very nature creates an 'us'- 'them' mentality and worldview. I am saved if I believe in an abide by this specific set of fundamentals like the 'rapture' and the 'second coming'. In fact, anyone who does not abide by them will not be saved. The world is divided between the 'saved' and the 'un-saved'. It is a kind of back door approach. I can convince myself that I am 'saved' if I believe that someone else is not 'saved', especially someone different than me in thought, word and belief. I am 'saved' because you are not and you are not like me. It is kind of an I am 'saved' and you are not, nanny-nanny, boo-boo mentality.

This explains why fundamentalists easily look down on others, and see others as evil and going to hell, anyone who is not exactly just like them. It helps relieve them also of any social or moral responsibility toward fellow humans. Why should I help someone who is only going to hell? They are going to hell for a reason; they are evil, and to help them would be going against the will of God. They use this as an excuse to ignore and reject the admonition of Jesus: "Whatever you do unto these the least of mine, you do unto me." That religion was invented to escape the terror of mortality is self- evident in the fact that religion which promises and 'afterlife' for a solution, an 'out' has to in turn, provide an 'out' for the 'out'. Whether fear of mortality or the fear of God's wrath or hell, anxiety, fear and terror foster's mental and emotional instability, paranoia, neurosis, sociopathology and severe mental disturbances. Perhaps religious fanaticism of a fundamentalist bent, should be considered a form of mental illness.

To take something on faith means to believe it without good reason, without fact, so by definition, a faith in the existence of supernatural entities clashes with reason. Lack of reasoning, for example, is reflected in the religious rationalization for suffering. Called Theodicy, according to which an all-powerful God had no choice but to allow epidemics and massacres killing tens of thousands, because a world without them is metaphysically impossible. Fundamentalists must never wonder what 'God's' plan was, what his intent was, when he created Adam and Eve in the "Garden of Eden". A 'heaven' right here on earth. Fundamentalists elevate some subjective, arbitrary moral good above the health, safety, and well-being of humans.

35

Examples would be accepting a divine savior, ratifying a sacred narrative i.e. 'the fundamentals', enforcing taboos, proselytizing other people to do the same, demonizing, punishing, even killing those who don't. They value fictitious 'souls' above real 'lives'. The fictitious above the real. This is a harsh, anxiety, fear and terror generating worldview to say the least.

Belief in an afterlife implies that health and happiness, the welfare of people in the here and now are not all that important, because life on earth is an infinitely small portion of one's 'existence'; that coercing people into accepting 'salvation' is doing them a favor even if you have to kill them; and that martyrdom may be the best thing that can ever happen to you. It makes it easy to not only ignore real pain and suffering on the part of others but to willfully contribute to it. Fundamentalist Christians share this magical thinking in common with the suicide bombers of ISIS, for example. For fundamentalists, heroic struggle, pursuing the struggle irrespective of means, costs or consequences to others, is the paramount reality, the greatest good, not the alleviating of or solving of human problems. Their hypocrisy is evident for example in the fact that while they reject science, they use computers instead of typewriters, cell phones instead of carrier pigeons, and have their surgery performed by science based surgical procedures rather than their preacher's magical incantations.

Fundamentalists reject the idea that reason and science can have anything to do with morality. They stake out a false claim. The idea that the ultimate good is to use knowledge to enhance human health, safety and welfare leaves fundamentalists dumb-founded. Deep explanations of the human condition and life unless they use theocratic psychobabble, 21st century voo-doo and magical thinking, they do not want to hear it. In fact, science is the morally enlightened enterprise, not religion. Science treats every human life as having equal value rather than privileging the people who are most like or closest to us or most attractive for some reason. Science holds out the hope

36

that we might identify the causes of suffering and pain; thereby, know which measures are most likely to reduce or eliminate them. Religion in contrast precludes this, because it fosters and thrives off of fear. It needs the existence of pain and suffering in order to survive. FDR was correct in his sense, in all spheres of human life, the greatest thing we have to fear is fear itself.

The escape from fear by way of ignorance and magical thinking engenders extreme paranoia, sociopathology and even more fear. The belief that an external force controls daily life fosters and exacerbates a shared paranoia among the tribe. Tornados, earthquakes, droughts, heat waves, wildfires, and hurricanes are believed to be signs and signals from God expressing his displeasure. They dropped lightening in general unless you get struck by it. Thus, the "boogeyman" of fear impacts every realm of life. Fear is the rock upon which religion, God and the after-life was founded and functions. The fear of mortality is replaced by the fear of God, God's wrath and hell. Sadomasochism is taking pleasure in the pain and abuse inflicted upon another person. If God wants to do something then he must be getting something out of it. God loves to cause fear and loves those who fear him. "The Lord taketh pleasure in them that FEAR him, in those that hope in his mercy." Psalm 147: 11.

"Praise ye the Lord. Blessed is the man that FEARETH the Lord, that delighteth greatly in his commandments." Psalm 112: 1. "Blessed is every one who FEARS the Lord, who walks in his ways." Psalm 128: 1. "Behold the eye of the Lord is upon them that FEAR him, upon them that hope in his mercy; to deliver their soul from death, and to keep them alive in famine." Psalm 33: 18-19. "Let all the earth FEAR the Lord; let all the inhabitants of the world stand in awe of him." Psalm 33: 8. "Therefore thou shalt keep the commandments of the Lord thy God, to walk in his ways, and to FEAR him." Deuteronomy 8: 6. "and now, Israel, what doeth the Lord they God require of thee, but to FEAR the Lord they God, to walk in all his ways, and to love him, and to serve the Lord thy

God with all thy heart and with all thy soul." Deuteronomy 10: 12.

"The friendship of the Lord is for those who FEAR him, and he makes known of them his covenant." Psalm 25: 14. "Come, ye children, hearken unto me: I will teach you the FEAR of the Lord." Psalm 34: 11. "Like as a father pitieth his children, so the Lord pitieth them that FEAR him, but the mercy of the Lord is from everlasting to everlasting upon them that FEAR him, and his righteousness unto children's children." Psalm 103: 13, 17. "Let them now that FEAR the Lord say, that his mercy endureth forever." Psalm 118: 4. Fundamentalists argue that "fear" means simply "respect." That it does not mean "cower in terror of punishment." They rationalize that it means "respect your elders", that it is like saying "honor your father because although he is just and stern, he is also wise and loving." So why would the Lord "pity" those for respecting him?

Respect is something that must be earned, and because the God of the old testament asserts his authority with powerful threats and actual acts of violence, "fear God" is thus being "frightened of his cruelty." The old testament most often connects fear of God with punishment, not earned respect. This is obvious in light of the fact that fear is used in relation to "mercy" very commonly. "Mercy" is compassionate or kindly forbearance shown toward an offender, an enemy, or other person in one's power; compassion, pity, or benevolence. So, if 'fear' was indeed 'respect' then why would one ask for or wish for God's "mercy" for "respecting" him?

"Sanctify the Lord of hosts himself, and let him be your FEAR, and let him be your DREAD". Isaiah 8: 13. "Therefore I am TERRIFIED at his presence, when I consider I am in DREAD of him. God has made my heart FAINT; the almighty has TERRIFIED me." Job 23:15-16. "Withdraw thine hand far from me and let not thy DREAD make me AFRAID." Job 13: 21. The prophets commonly preached and preachers yet today preach "The Wrath of God", and yet to say "fear" means "respect" or anything else than

FEAR, is out and out laughable. It is just another example of the illogic, irrationality and insanity of fundamentalist religions ('God the Most Unpleasant Character in All Fiction', Dan Barker). Humanity's fear of death is transformed through the denial of death into many illogical and irrational fears and belief systems which in turn generate innumerable never ending human problems, pain, and suffering. Humanity becomes his own worse enemy and he is not 'saved' from a damned thing, not even himself!

Part Two

The Dream

Jesus of the Gospels knew that the fear of death disguised itself in many irrational and illogical fears in everyday life. He kept this in mind when he taught and preached an alternative wisdom and alternative life style. Jesus rejected fear as the basis of relationships. The Old Testament was written before him and the New Testament was written years after him. He had nothing to do, personally with their writing. The 'far religious right' today offers up little more than the rote mouthing of scriptures, sugary nostalgia and platitudes with an abundant amount of fear for just about everything. Jesus preached as declared by Paul, that "Love is the fulfilling of the Law," and, as declared by Peter "Above all things have fervent love among yourselves" (above all things, even faith!). And, as John declared Jesus saying, "God is love." Jesus, in the parable of the Good Samaritan, said that; "Love is above all law." The 'far religious right' knows only fear and hate. If God is love, then fear or hate in any form or fashion should not exist or appear, and should not be part of in any way, religion or religious beliefs.

For the 'far religious right', anti-intellectualism for example, remains strongly entrenched and is grounded in fear not faith. The ongoing suspicion that scientific discoveries or rigorous biblical scholarship will undermine faith is a tacit admission that faith is threatened by knowledge, because it is ultimately constructed on weak or faulty beliefs and, like a house of cards, needs to be protected from collapsing. Out of fear, they rally and campaign to get legislators elected who will pass legislation based on and enforcing the scriptures. They insist on nothing less than a punishing, vindictive, retributive, fear-inducing criminal justice system. They insist on the passing of legislation to force their edicts and notions of morality on everyone else. They are not aware of the admonition of Benjamin Franklin that if your religion needs government to hold it up, then it must really suck!

Not knowing Jesus, the 'far religious right' does not know that the peddling of fear in any form as incentive to faith remains the most offensive sin that can be committed in the name of Jesus. He was and is, and will always be about compassion, pure, reckless compassion, and not fear or hate. Many people thought that Jesus was insane. In Mark 3: 21, his family heard of his casting out of demons and heard of the unruly crowds who followed him and went out to restrain him because people were saying; "He has gone out of his mind." Jesus only appeared to be mad. In fact, so does any one who is both fully alive and radically free from convention. Persons who think and act differently appear crazy only because the conventional wisdom of their age is so fully and unthinkingly accepted by everyone, that any challenge to it what so ever, appears desperate. In fact, it is as Thoreau in Walden states; "it is mass resignation that is the true desperation."

A life of unbridled radical freedom is a life lived outside the shackles of anxiety and fear that controls most of us. It is a way of being in the world that is so fully connected to another source of wisdom and worthiness that the person appears to be "out of it" or missing something. This also was in part what Jesus meant when he said that he was "in this world, but not of it." Thoreau said: "The mass of men live lives of quiet desperation, what is called resignation is confirmed desperation." What is "missing" is the despair that Soren Keirkegaard called the "sickness unto death," that gnawing angst that shadows all our days. It entails the angst addressed by Marin Heidegger in "Being and Time." We try in vain to secure ourselves against our own insecurity, and thus, we never become a "self." We are finite, vain, and consumed with the fear of death, as well as the fear it will overwhelm us, if we do not stay busy managing the demands of modern life.

As if possessed by a desire to upend the status quo in which he was raised and bring down the judgement of the very faith he sought to reform, Jesus did it fearlessly and counselled his followers to "fear not." Knowing that fear is the enemy of the moral life, Jesus attacked the sacred cows of his day and strongly challenged conventional wisdom. The wisdom of Jesus drove his critics to fear that the very foundations of society was being destroyed and the advantages of the righteous were being mocked. His life and teachings still scare the smell out of fundamentalists and legalists, yet today. He taught, for example, that there was no final judgement in God's unconditional love. There is nothing more frightening to the 'far religious right' than the notion that there is no final judgement. There are passages in the scriptures about a final judgement, but they are the refrains of Mathew's more legalistic view, and his strong attachment to Mosaic Law.

When Jesus brought up such final judgements, it was to subvert conventional beliefs about those judgements. Jesus's wisdom is still today a threat to law and order, to the religious establishment, and to the social hierarchy that creates and preserves wealth. It is the antithesis to the 'far religious right.' Christianity is the only major religious tradition whose founder was executed by established authority. It was what Jesus did that marked him out for death. He provided a role model and a demonstration toward a viable alternative life and reality. Those who challenge the status quo, and do so with bold conviction and inspiring charisma, are at risk of being executed. Albert Schweitzer lamented: "What has been passing for Christianity during these nineteen centuries is full of weaknesses and mistakes, not springing from the spirit of Jesus." Jesus's was the pre-Christian wisdom of a Galilean Sage of the peasant class. Jesus was Jewish and spoke as a Jewish man to Jewish followers. This made him dangerously effective in recruiting followers.

In order to put down a growing rebellion that Jesus was inspiring, Rome executed him with the help of Jewish proxies, establishment dupes, who did not represent the Jews but carried out the orders of the authorities. The 'far religious right' would do the same thing today. Jesus entertained no status in the eyes of the establishment. According to Luke, Jesus's family came from Nazareth but traveled to Bethlehem because of the census. Jesus is born on the road, as a refugee, and finally returns to Nazareth.

44

But he spent most of his life as a nomad, similar to the life of an immigrant, in search of a home. To reiterate, Jesus was a lower-class Jew, born a Jew in poverty, died a Jew in poverty and his only scripture was the Hebrew Bible. Jesus spoke as a Jew to fellow Jews, all of his first followers were Jewish, and so were all the authors of the New Testament. Jesus practiced social justice, spoke with women, did not shy away from the unclean, taught nonviolence, and cared for the poor and the marginalized. He was not an exception to the Jewish rule. Jesus became a woodworker, a tekton in Greek, which is not in any strict sense a carpenter, but one who made wood products like doors, roof beams, furniture, boxes, etc. He was at the lower end of the peasant class. In the Greco-Roman world, peasants lived at the subsistence level, barely able to support their own farming efforts, and they were required to send two-thirds of their annual crop to support the upper class. It was an early version of today's "trickle down" or "supply side" economics supported today by the 'far religious right.'

Jesus was dirt poor, living just a notch above the degraded outcasts, untouchables, and expendables, the slaves, beggars, and day laborers. However, Jesus was wise. He was charismatic, a gifted speaker and story teller. He was a teacher of wisdom who dreamed of a better world. His dream was to bring about that better world right here on earth in the here and now. He taught opposition to tradition and convention. Both his life and his message were subversive. Jesus was so grounded in compassion that he could not be around the sick or the broken without attempting to heal them. His compassion is totally incomprehensible to today's 'religious far right.' What Jesus taught was subversive wisdom.

Jesus led followers away from both convention and clinging to authoritative proclamations and dictates, to enlightenment and compassion. Being wise for Jesus meant teaching subversive ideas in a subversive manner. He trapped listeners inside their own instincts for the truth, forcing them to appropriate it through a struggle to reduce their own cognitive dissonance. Their own beliefs created the horrible world around them. His use of aphorisms, short wisdom sayings is one example, but his primary teaching method was use of the parable. He taught that a new society to be called the Kingdom of God could be experienced now, as an alternative to Roman power. Jesus told his disciples to "learn from me." This was a call to establish a community of alternative commitments and social practices, a communal or communistic society.

The French word "commune" appeared in the 12th century from the Medieval Latin word "communia," meaning a large gathering of people sharing a common life; from Latin "communis," things held in common. Jesus lived his adult life as a nomad, his only property a robe and sandals. Jesus spent his adult life living and traveling around with twelve men. They lived a communal life. His was a social and theological challenge to Roman oppression. The Gospel of Jesus is an amazingly radical political statement buried under centuries of misconceptions, misunderstandings, reactionary and sentimental interpretations. The society of the "Kingdom of God" was to be constructed around radical egalitarian principles, a new economic system based on need, not greed, in which violence and oppression in any form is rejected and all social divisions of the economic world are rejected.

Jesus was a first-century Mediterranean Jewish peasant, refugee, and nomad, who lived more like an immigrant than a rooted citizen, a teacher of wisdom, a social prophet, and movement founder. His principle teaching tool was the parable, and he knew the hard sayings of the Jewish prophets who proceeded him. Jesus had a vision, and a dream. He dreamed of the "Kingdom of God" to be created right here on earth and created by persons in relationship to one another. It is stated in the Lord's prayer; "Thy Kingdom come, thy will be done ('done' like 'do' is intensively active) on earth as it is in heaven." The covenant here is that this "will" will be 'done' by our faithful effort to make it happen. This would of course disrupt the established status quo of wealth. The biblical covenant is egalitarian, social, communal, and it is communistic. It would need no formal government as Marx stated: "and the state as we know it will whither away." And along with it, the oligarchy of the capitalist status quo will wither away. It is the ever-present fear of Wall-Street.

Jesus told his disciples to seek the truth. Truth is fact; it is based on and reflects knowledge, not mere belief, superstition, myth. When we know and trust what is going on, we enjoy more fully all aspects of being human, the good and the bad. We can set the stage for true emotions that we know will be good for us. We can only do this by creating human communities un-encumbered by belief. To simply "believe" is not to "know" anything. By "Knowing," we can build the kind of loving, secular community that can heal broken lives and transform all of us and our children into better, happier people. Compassion and community should be synonymous. The idea of a congregation without a church, religion, or even a God is not an oxymoron. Congregation is a word that strongly evokes a certain kind of community, a really close knit, strong community that can make strong change happen in the world.

Jesus's church is a church of compassion, not religion where things like acceptance is compassion. Two very startling things arrest us in John's version of the future (Revelation/The Gospel of John). The first is that the most similar thing to heaven he could think of was a city; the second, that there was no church in that city. Almost nothing more revolutionary could be said, even to the modern world, in the name of religion. No church-that is the defiance of religion; a city-that is the antipodes of heaven. Yet John combines these contradictions in one daring image and holds up to the world the picture of a city without a church as his ideal of the heavenly life ('The City Without a Church', Henry Drummond). Now that would be quite a place indeed, a community, a society, without a church or a government! Let freedom ring!

Without the collective, without society, humans would not even develop normally as humans as in the case of the "feral child." Indeed, they may not even live long, normal, productive lives let alone achieve anything beyond. One is reminded of Genie (the pseudonym for an American feral child), who was a victim of severe abuse, neglect, and social isolation. Starting at the age of 20 months, her father kept her as socially isolated as possible. Until she reached the age of 13 years and 7 months, he kept her locked alone in a room. The extent of her isolation prevented her from being exposed to any significant amount of speech, and as a result, she did not acquire language during her childhood. Her abuse came to the attention of Los Angeles child welfare authorities on November 4, 1970 ('Genie: A Scientific Tragedy' (2 ed., Russ Rymer; Susan Curtiss, et.al., 'Genie: A Psycholinquistic Study of a Modern-Day "Wild Child", 'Perspectives in Neurolinquistics and Psycholinquistics').

Human life is all about relationships, so is God and the Kingdom of God, relationships of unconditional love. Yes, there is a "prosperity" Gospel, and the question is to what are we supposed to "prosper" to or in? Jesus tells us to be "in this world" but "not of it," just as he is. "Not of it' - tells us we are not to prosper in material things, mammon, but in spiritual things like our relationships with fellow persons. Also, we find it in Jesus's telling his disciples to take "no bread, no bag, no money in their belts"- (Mark 6: 8) as they go forth to 'prosper'; yes, they were to 'prosper' in "spirit," in "faith," not wealth.

As reiterated in Matthew; 6: 19-20; "Do not store up for yourselves treasures on earth..." To prosper in spirit is to prosper in our relationships with other people. The very essence, the very foundation of our humanness which gives us the ability to bring about the Kingdom of God right here on earth in the here and now, is our capacity for empathizing with each other and for unconditional love. Yes, it is all about relationships. Symbolic Interaction theory holds that humans literally create, change

48

or maintain themselves, each other and reality in the process of constant, ongoing symbolic interaction between them. What could be more entailing of "God is Love", if those interactions were expressions of pure unconditional love, commitment, respect, empathy, responsibility and caring. This is totally alien, incomprehensible, foreign, to the fundamentalist mind.

Capitalism requires us to treat people as "things", indeed as "commodities", not humans. Job seekers are told that they must "sell" themselves to potential employers like a pound of hamburger on the meat shelf. In capitalist economies, all human relations are calculated on the individual's "bottom line," all relations are economic, practical, pragmatic, plutonic. In addition, with formal government dominated by powerful elites ('Testing Theories of American Politics: Elites, Interest Groups, and Average Citizens.' Martin Gilens and Benjamin I. Page, The Umbrella of legalism is imposed and intertwined with the economic order. Therefore, society Jesus dreamed of, the "Kingdom of God" cannot exist under such conditions. This is why Jesus was calling for a communal or communist society in the genre of what Marx called "Modern Communism," where neither a formal, legalistic, government (oppressive by its very nature), or capitalistic government exists. The early disciples mirrored this society. They were a collection of self-selected misfits who tramped around the country living a communal life and practiced radical hospitality. 'Privilege' was unknown to them and they recognized it not.

Jesus was a vagrant, a Rabbi always on the go. Jesus left his native Galilee, crossed Judea and Sumeria and even ventured into foreign territory. Jesus did not set up shop in Jerusalem or near a rabbinical school. His preference was for the uncertainty of the road rather than the security of an institution. It is clear that he erected a creative distance from traditions and old customs. Jesus's life and thoughts comprise the entire capital of someone on the move, of a migrant. Jesus was "the common people he met on the road." This is captured in the words of poet Henri Michaux: "I am a crowd". Jesus would add: "and the crowd is I". "Wherever two or more of you are gathered in my name, so there I will be". Jesus lived a life which could be called the poverty of open hands to show that one does not possess anything.

The first people of the Old Testament were nomads and the first Christians were called people of "the way". Movement is at the heart of the biblical message. After Abraham heard the order "Go from your country and your kindred and your father's house to the land that I will show you" (Gen 12), setting out on a journey became a way of life, a lifestyle for God's friends. The command "Go", runs clear through the two testaments. The command meant literally, "go to, or for, yourself," leave for your benefit and for your good. The adventures of Christ, his disciples and early Christians demonstrate the rhythm of this kind of life; the life of a nomad, the life of an immigrant, the life of a refugee. Comprised of departures and returns, attachments and detachments, their lives were structured according to the rhythm; leave, settle down, leave again. It was a life unattached to the material world and relationships were everything.

Jesus's nomadic lifestyle, which began before his birth, has nothing of fantasy or pleasure seeking about it. He subscribed to a long tradition. Taking to the road resolutely was the following of a call, an intuition, a questioning. This nomadic lifestyle fosters a scaling down, not only of possessions but of our habits. Jesus would say this (most) enriches us. The wandering rabbi knew that God's self-revelation plainly expresses movement: "I will be who I will be". And God expects that we too will be willing to do so. "Churches without Walls" are nomadic churches (followers) following the nomad of Nazareth, who was never where he was supposed to be, and who would arrive out of the blue and leave in the same way. This is necessitated of course to some degree when the authorities are after you.

The vagrant Jesus traversed across mountains and through

valleys, passing from the water to dry ground, from the plain to the hilltop, from town to countryside, without glitz, without glamour, without noise, money or property, bathed only in sunlight. The Gospels are movement, journey. They recount more than once the story of a man who leaves on a trip. We are not told where he goes; he just leaves. He leaves for a long time and leaves behind anything he had. (Matthew 25: 14; Mark 13: 33-36). Rather than taking advantage of his position of power, he delegates responsibilities to others and clears the way for solidarity and dignity, acts of sharing and trust. What Jesus was concerned about for his friends was fear itself, that fear that leads to an inability to enter into the movement of life.

To follow the roving Rabbi of Nazareth is to join his school, to learn to speak his language, to act with his feet, his body, in his way; the road becomes school, we sow open handedly to all four winds. The life of a nomad, immigrant, refugee, rich with experience, is an education. It reflects what John Dewey meant by education as organizing the materials of experience. On the road, Jesus was a friend of prostitutes and collaborators, a rabbi, a Jew, a story teller, a man of Galilee, a carpenter's son, a righter of wrongs, a teacher, an agitator. One can almost hear him say; "follow me and keep up!"

Luke tells about how this person who would become an itinerant rabbi, and vagrant, spending his entire adult life living and traveling around with twelve men, was first a kid. Jesus was a kid who traveled, a migrant child continually on the move, a nomad even in the womb. From the moment of his conception, this future roving rabbi from Nazareth, this perpetual vagrant, would not stay put. His mother got up and set off in haste, with the child in her womb, over the mountain to a little village in Judea to see her cousin. Before even setting foot on earth, Jesus crossed the Judean hills. It was the harsh countryside he would in the future travel up and down relentlessly.

The child, yet to be born, and his parents became refugees when they had to leave their village of Nazareth. They crossed the hills of Judea on the edge of the wilderness to the village of Bethlehem. Later, they went home at last to their village of Nazareth, in the hills of Galilee. Jesus had been born on the road, a refugee. In his childhood, he liked to run all over the countryside with his friends. Later, Jesus began his work as an itinerant rabbi ceaselessly traveling, ceaselessly meeting with women, men and children of all sorts and conditions, but with a preference for the poor, the sick, the marginalized, those who lost their place in society.

Jesus loved the individuals who crossed his path, and he was not afraid of engaging in relationships that would shock. It would cause the 'far religious right' today to go into convulsions. As Will Rogers once said: "I never met a man I did not like." Sinners, collaborators, prostitutes, members of the occupation, and dropouts of all sorts had claim on his undivided attention and friendship. He showed infinite respect to women and the sick, as well as to Samaritans and Romans. With incredible freedom his empathy and sympathy, like his friendship, knew no discrimination, or rejection, or boundaries. The 'far religious right' today holds those who Jesus called "the least of mine" in great disdain as "no-goods," "welfare cheats" and "bums too lazy to work." They elect politicians who wage war on them and make life as difficult as possible, regardless if they are children, the elderly, the handicapped, it makes no matter. People from Galilee whose accent was often sneered at, toll collectors, craftsmen, easy women, all were what came to be called his disciples. Following Jesus was literally walking behind him, in his footsteps, over the roads of Samaria, into the Judean hills, or along the Galilean Seashore. Their school was roaming around, moving about, going from place to place. Their school was trust as they shared the unpredictability of daily life. This way of life focused on wondering across plains and over hills. It was demanding. Jesus tramped from town to town, and then on to another, from one seashore to another. Sometimes for rest, he was happy with a field or a meadow.

With nothing but a robe and sandals, he was always ready at any moment, any time of day or night, to get on the road. The rabbi from Nazareth could not stay put and did not want to. Jesus's life is the ultimate example of being "in" the world, but not "of it". As once sung by Janice Joplin, "Freedom is just another word for nothing left to lose." This life knows little fear, if any. ('Jesus of Nazareth Always on The Move', Christianne Meroz). It is the kind of freedom that Jesus envisioned for all of humankind in his dream of bringing about the "Kingdom of God." One could say that Jesus of Nazareth, the roving rabbi, itinerate preacher and vagrant "lived" Christianity. Jesus demonstrated what would be "Christian" relationships with fellow persons and expected nothing less from his followers.

If Christianity has anything even remotely to do with Jesus Christ and aspects of concrete everyday life like the health, safety and welfare of people, it would have a formidable impact on contemporary life. This would be true only if truly believed in and seriously practiced by those who 'claim' to be Christians. With over two billion followers, Christianity is the most widespread religion and constitutes almost one third of the world's population. Since the time of Christ, criticisms of Christianity, as practiced, have almost always stemmed from or been linked to the concrete aspects of everyday life. One can understand for example, Karl Marx's criticism of 'establishment' (state) religion or 'church' because during Marx's time, powerful Christian nations (in which capitalism was taking hold) of Western Europe justified colonial expansion and exploitation by claiming that they were only and "dutifully" "converting heathens." They even used Christianity to justify the stealing of land and belongings, and the slaughter of women and children, in order to achieve conversion.

Today, for example, most churches throughout the U.S. still remain significantly segregated, and this is a reflection of the fact that major religions and churches in the South still believe that the enslavement of blacks is consistent with God's will. Even a superficial study of the life of Christ shows it to be a life of involvement, a life focused on the concrete realities of everyday life, an ethical and moral focus on the here and now. For example, Luke's beatitudes are stated in terms of economic status and class: "Blessed are you the poor, for yours is the Kingdom of God, but woe to you that are rich!" (48). Jesus's life was unquestioningly a life punctuated by morality and ethics. Jesus Christ was a radical cultural critic and ethicist.

Christ's actions constituted the core message, a message of liberation. His was a life impassioned with a revolutionary fervor. The message for his true followers of whatever Christian denomination is a message of liberation theology. It is a clear and straightforward simple message: Oppression of any kind, in any amount, runs counter to Christian morality. Oppression is preventable, and as such, it is a matter of faith, duty and social justice that Christians must act to promote and bring about greater social equality, and the elimination of oppression be it economic, political or social.

Liberation theology has been defined as: 'A fusion of Christian principles with Marxism or with political activism of a Marxist character.' This definition was created in modern times by powerful and wealthy elites to deliberately discredit Jesus's liberation theology. By doing this, it made Jesus's liberation theology 'safe' (unacceptable) by attaching Marx's name to them. Marx deserves no credit what so ever for or connection to liberation theology, the practical religion of Jesus Christ. Obviously, Marx came centuries after Jesus clearly elaborated its message in his sermon on the mount. This is why thousands of years ago, in Jerusalem, Jesus Christ was tried and sentenced to be crucified on charges that he was a threat to established political, economic, and religious leaders.

This is why in Jewish writings we are told quite specifically and accurately: "He (Jesus) was a revolutionary." The Talmud says: "On the eve of the Passover Jesus of Nazareth was crucified. During forty days a forerunner went before him crying aloud: "He ought to be stoned because he practiced magic, has led Israel astray, and caused them to rise in rebellion." As Morton Smith in 'The Secret Gospel, the Discovery and Interpretation of The Secret Gospel, according to Mark,' tells us that: "Mark's story of Jesus' last days of liberty and his arrest (Mark 14: 12-52) reads like something from the adventures of a revolutionist."

"According to him, Jesus had created some sort of disturbance in the Jerusalem temple and the high priests who were also the city authorities, were waiting for a chance to arrest him privately, when the arrest would not likely cause a riot. He, therefore, came into the city only by day with the crowds and spent the nights in a village near the desert from which he could escape if any troops were seen coming." Harry Fosdick in 'The Man from Nazareth' points out: "He (Jesus) was gathering disciples, sending them out on missions, attracting a popular following, launching a movement. This man intended insurrection." Fosdick goes on to state: "Such was the man the Pharisees confronted, out to do something radical and revolutionary in Israel."

Colonel V. Donner in his book 'The Samaritan Strategy' points out: "Christ took the ultimate political position of his day. He challenged the existing order and announced a new government, The Kingdom of God, with himself as its head. During Christ's lifetime, the Roman Empire believed that the ultimate God was the Roman State and the Roman Empire. Refusing to worship the emperor was considered an act of atheism and treason, punishable by death. Since the Roman government combined its political power of government with an official religion of emperor worship, to defy the state (in effect, a theocracy) was both a political offense and a religious heresy." Donner goes on to explain: "When Christ stated that he, not Caesar, had been given all authority in heaven and earth by God, and that God's laws had precedence over Caesar's edicts, Christ challenged the political and spiritual authority of the world's government. He and his followers committed the ultimate rebellious political act: treasonous rebellion against the foundations of the state."

The beginning of Christianity was beyond political. It was revolutionary. Jesus's critique encompassed not just the political and religious status quo, but all of society and culture of his day. Marcus Borg in the preface of 'The Lost Gospel Q, The Original Saying of Jesus', reminds us that: "He (Jesus) was a radical cultural critic. Though subversion of cultural consciousness is characteristic of most teachers of unconventional wisdom, there is also sharp and passionate social criticism in Q. It is directed against wealth and against the ruling elites (religious, political and economic) Indeed, the Jesus of Q threatens Jerusalem (the home of the elites) with divine judgement. The social passion of Jesus's radical cultural criticism makes him similar to the great social prophets of the Hebrew Bible."

The response to Jesus was guaranteed by his own actions. In 'Crucify Him', Dale Foreman discusses the trial of Jesus: "In the tradition of later political show trials, Jesus was labeled by his enemies and framed for ideological reasons. But by claiming to be both God and man, he was, in a sense, too much for any one legal system to handle. So, after being accused of both religious and political crimes, he was tried in the legal systems of two cultures. The political crime was that of causing people to riot, insurrection. The Sanhedrin not having the power to put a criminal to death, accused Jesus of sedition, that is plotting the violent overthrow of the Roman government in Judea, so that the Romans would be forced to execute him."

In studying the actions and words of Christ, one realizes that Jesus was a master revolutionary. He was extremely adept at calling for a revolution, without from a legal standpoint calling for a revolution. This is why, as Forman points out, he was actually found innocent on the political charges. At Jesus's political show-trial the authorities did, however, perceive and believe him to be a revolutionist. Jesus of course had a unique edge that no revolutionary has had since. How do you safely discredit someone who claims to be the Son of God, especially when a significant number of people believe him? Fosdick is quite correct when he points out that: "Jesus was not primarily a teacher, he was a reformer. He came not only to say something but to do something, whatever else was in his mind, this much was there, and it made of him not so much a rabbi, as an active reformer insisting on change."

However, Fosdick erroneously tries to argue that Jesus did not personally want revolutionary change but, instead, wanted evolutionary change. What Fosdick overlooks is that while Jesus may not have tried so much personally and individually to cause change, to reconstruct society, change the economic system and other things, it was his personal, individual mission to move the masses to do it. And Jesus did not want a long drawn-out evolutionary process. The strength and speed with which Jesus was pushing for change quickly ushered in his execution in his early thirties. As Fosdick himself points out: "He (Jesus) was certainly a reformer, he would not give the status quo in Israel a moment's rest. At one point after another he attacked it the economic evils of proud and greedy wealth, the social evils of class prejudice, the ruthless tyranny of rulers, the blasphemy of commercialism, the unfairness to women, and with tireless rigor and insistence the religious failures of Pharisaic legalism (a point ignored by today's legalistic Christians.) Moreover, whenever the opportunity opened, he not only talked but acted."

It does not sound by any stretch of the imagination to this writer that this suggests Jesus was looking for evolutionary rather than revolutionary change. Perhaps something in between, but certainly something far more revolutionary than evolutionary. There was a reason why Jesus often posted guards on watches. Jesus, indeed among other things, spoke out against the econom-

57

ic evils of wealth, the evils of class prejudice and considered commercialism as nothing less than out and out blasphemy. Capitalism today, on the other hand, is a secular religion that worships wealth, fosters class prejudice, and holds commercialism sacred. The economic and social position of Jesus in relation to capitalism makes him, especially, economically a Marxian communist in comparison. Fundamentalists glorify capitalism and wealth and sit in the front pew of the secular religion of capitalism.

Jesus spent his life calling people to action in his revolution. As Foreman states: "A (true) follower of Jesus is called upon to stand up publicly for the truth regardless of cost. The Christian is asked to make a difference, to leave the world a better place with every new generation. The (true) believer is expected to participate in the institutions of the time, to meet people where they live, the ultimate responsibility is ours." Jesus himself warns us, should we not follow his example in Rev. 22: 12, "Behold, I am coming soon, bringing my recompense, to repay everyone for what he HAS DONE." Most Christians today go to great lengths and mental gymnastics to avoid their responsibility. They become fundamentalist evangelicals, born again Christians. They want to have their cake and eat it too. They want simple "outs" that allow them to pretend to be Christians without actually having to do anything. They are easily recognized. For example: "The Bible is all you need to know" or "People just need to pray."

They insist on taking the Bible literally, word for word as inerrant and that is the way it was. Only a full-blown Schizophrenic could make any sense out of a literal interpretation of the Bible. In fact, a literal interpretation of the Bible is not only erroneous but dangerous, as demonstrated by the likes of ISIS. Christian fundamentalists have the exact same mentality. Biblical scholars point out that no one has a letter-by-letter version of the Bible as originally written. No one. It simply does not exist. Even the oldest surviving writings include variations of the original. Over 2,700 years old, it was written by different au-

58

thors at different times. It was subject to revision and interpretation by many different special interests over and over again.

Literalists rely heavily on the "second coming", which in their mind means, I don't really need to do anything but sit back, pray, and wait for Jesus to come get me. I know there is a heaven and I am going there. That is a real dandy. These people probably think that 'Miss Piggy' is a real person. They set sail everyday in their own mind on the good ship 'lollipop' and complain about the evil seas they let rage around them. Hell, they vote for them. Many of them have been "born again" a religious absurdity picked from the scriptures with a tweezers. Jesus used the words born again one single time in his entire life. He directed those words to the heretic Nicodemus (a Pharisee and member of the Sanhedrin) not to his disciples.

One would think that if something was so important, so vital that it determined whether one went to heaven or not, that Jesus would have impressed it on his disciples. He would tell them, preach it to them. He would certainly repeat it often. Jesus said "born again" one single time and then only directed it to Nicodemus, no one else. Jesus was frustrated with this heretic to the point of telling him that he was so far off track that he would have to start all over again i.e. be born again to get back on track. "Born again" Christians take this and make it the paramount thing in the scriptures. All else is practically irrelevant. They are so convinced of this that they literally take anything else that Jesus said and twist and re-interpret it in their own mind to mean "born again". If Jesus had said: I "gotta" pee, they would say, see! Jesus is telling us we must be born again. That is what he is saying.

Capitalism has evolved into a far more anti-Christian antagonistic system to the teachings of Jesus than the Roman Empire ever was or could have been. Capitalism goes beyond the political, economic and social to the very rationality and consciousness of humankind. It strips humanity of even having the possibility of having any value other than the value of a 'thing'. It strips humans of humanity itself. Indeed, it does effectively make a person a mindless biological consuming robot, a 'thing.' Yet, the "far religious right" glorifies wealth and capitalism. In 'Money and the Meaning of Life,' Jacob Needleman points out: "What Weber ('The Protestant Ethic and the Spirit of Capitalism') saw was not only capitalism. What he saw was capitalism made into a religion, a religion in the service of which man employed all the gifts of his mind and heart. And thus, he argued, came from the leakage into the outer life of the inner spirit of a form of the Christian religion known as Protestantism (Specifically, 17th Century Calvinist Doctrine)."

Entailed in this, is the externalization and objectification of the human spirit and all its traits. Each person becomes more and more an object, a thing (a commodity), an empty shell of humanity at best, devoid of internal value. Thus, to have any value at all, he is forced to look for it externally in things. Things and, inanimate objects, define, validate, and give value to a person's existence. Needleman argues that: "The hell of modern man is the philosophy of avarice. Weber saw man writhing in a hell ruled by the money demon. That (man's) energy and the commitment, the blind passion of this all-to-palpable phantasm called money, the energy to organize his whole communal life on earth for the sake of the perpetual acquisition of money."

In order for profit, as a human value, to increase, (in geometric proportions) other human values, especially any opposing values like true Christian values found in the life and teachings of Jesus Christ, or democratic values, must be diminished in direct proportion to them. As Needleman writes: "Who spends all his time and all his private energies, who dreams and fashions his values and ideals, who, in short, gives all his substance, to the making of money? Man! His life on earth dedicated to, to what? Manufacturing, marketing, investing! Man! Possessed of a power of mind that called him to conceive and think rationally about the whole essence of creation and God's order, who can work to grasp the laws of life and matter, who is called to ponder and participate in the essence of divinity itself and yet who uses his specifically human power of mind for the ultimate aim of: gathering money!"

Jesus did not want what today has become known as religion. Nothing he said or did suggests it. Perhaps he foresaw the eventual rise of the religion of capitalism and free enterprise and the fusing of capitalism with Christian religion into one. Perhaps his efforts were at least in part to prevent the development and rise of capitalist religion. Capitalism and its free enterprise system (free to rape, plunder and pillage humanity itself), is without any doubt what so ever, the most destructive and consuming force of humanity ever devised by humankind. Under capitalism we have already (1) Accepted putting a price tag on human life, (2) That the price is negotiable; and thus, (3) That if the price is negotiable then trade-offs are possible (and acceptable) and; thus, that the value of humans and human life are tradable (interchangeable) with other "things". What kind of morality does this thinking reflect? Because of 1, 2 and 3, then a cost-benefit analysis can be applied to the value of human life. By implication then; (4) Human life is "dispensable". Finally, if human life is dispensable, then logically it is sellable and buyable which is exactly the attitude capitalism has toward it.

Look at the characteristics of capitalism that have been adopted by churches. More and more, religions and churches are engaging in aggressive competitive "marketing". That's right, marketing! The selling of religion. They are engaging in intense ad campaigns with ads showing up everywhere from public restrooms to bars. Newspaper and magazine ads, radio and television ads and services, web sites, cable outlets all suggest that establishment religion is having some serious problems when they, in effect, become retailers, when they have to "market" and "sell" God. It is telling that recently, among a group of businessmen, an ordained minister in a completely serious

61

tone, continually and only referred to himself as the "CEO" of his church. He never once used "pastor" or "minister" to refer to himself or his position in the church. Preachers of the "far religious right" try to make Jesus out to be a wall-street tycoon and tell us like Joel Osteen that Jesus wants us to be rich!

Since the very beginning of civilization humankind has dealt with two fundamental problems. One, how to produce those things he needed for survival and two, how should those things once produced by society be distributed? The first person to challenge, in any serious way, the problem of distribution of society's production (today commonly referred to as the GNP, Gross National Product) was Jesus Christ. This challenge automatically classified him as a radical. Jesus grounded his attack of the distribution problem on traditional religious beliefs and teachings as well as his modifications of those teachings. Without a doubt, Jesus came down heavily and almost exclusively on the side of equality leaving very little if any room for any inequality at all.

In fact, Jesus was the world's first egalitarian in word and deed. This is why an Oklahoma minister once lamented: "It is impossible to talk about Jesus without making him sound like a communist." Jesus addressed the question of production by calling for a highly limited consumption. For example, in Timothy 6: 6,8,9: "But godliness with contentment is great gain and having food and raiment let us be therewith content. But they that will be rich fall into temptation and a snare, and into many foolish and hurtful lusts, which drown men in destruction and perdition." Coming also in the 'back door', Jesus again deals with the question of distribution by limiting consumption and thus production to only those things that are absolutely necessary to sustain a very modest life and nothing more.

Why? Because the production of anything beyond what is needed to sustain life engenders greed. Think about it. Greed is the only thing left that over production can engender because it is not really needed for anything else. Jesus knew also that greed produces inequality that is destructive of morality and humanity. Thus, "But they that will be rich fall into temptation and a snare and into many foolish and hurtful lusts, which drown men in destruction and perdition." The puritan regulated himself under traditional capitalism, but the economic system which 17th Century Calvinist Doctrine created, modern capitalism, cannot and does not, allow self-regulation to any significant extent. Self-regulation cannot be engaged in under modern unlimited capitalism. As Tawny ('Religion and the Rise of Capitalism') well recognized: "There can be no compromise."

Jesus Christ was one of the first persons on earth to command care for the poor, the orphans, and the suffering. If you read the Sermon on the Mount of Jesus Christ, and the moral Code of the Builder of Communism, they are very similar and compatible. The general intent is identical. To paraphrase from The Moral Code of the Builder, 1961; You should work hard for the good of society, so everyone, not just you, can benefit. Doing what is best for everyone should be very important. You should never do or support anything that is not good for everyone. People should not just care about themselves. Everyone should care about everyone else. Everyone should help each other. Every person support society, and society support every person. "collectivism and comradely mutual assistance; one for all and all for one." People should respect each other and be good to each other; every man is a friend, comrade, and brother to every other man. You should always be honest, do the right things and be humble.

The code goes on to address the family: all family members should respect each other. Raising children should be important to everyone. You should never accept things that are not fair; people who do not do their fair share; people who are not honest; or people who try to get ahead and make money just for themselves. All people in the USSR should treat each other like friends and brothers. You should never treat someone badly because of the country they are from or because of their race. Thus, the code also addresses race relations. Going all the way back to mono-worshippers of Zoroaster, almost all religious movements have the same main communistic idea which is, love our neighbor as yourself. This strongly reflects and parallels Jesus's final command to his disciples: "Love one another as I have loved you."

Certainly, some of the most key concepts in Marx's thinking were; capital, private property, class and equality. The flip side of the question was Jesus Christ a communist? Is the question, did Marx get his seminal ideas from Jesus Christ? Considering class and equality: "There is neither Jew nor Greek, there is neither bond nor free, there is neither male nor female: for ye are all one in Jesus Christ." (Galatians 3: 28). Jesus's attitudes regarding capital and private property are clear: "Carry neither purse, nor scrip, nor shoes." (Luke 10: 4). And, "for (I mean) not that other men be eased, and ye be burdened. But by an equality, (that) now at this time 'your' abundance (may be a supply) for their want, that 'their' abundance also may be (a supply) for 'your' want, that there may be equality. As it is written, he that (had gathered) little had no lack." (Corinthians 11; 8: 13-15).

Considering capital: "for it is easier for a camel to go through a needle's eye, than for a rich man to enter the Kingdom of God." (Luke 18: 25). "If thou wilt be perfect, go (and) sell that thou hast, and give to the poor." (Matthew 19: 21). "How hardly shall they that have riches enter into the Kingdom of God." (Mark 10: 23). "How hard is it for them that trust in riches to enter into the Kingdom of God." (Mark 10: 24). "No servant can serve two masters: for either he will hate the one and love the other; or else he will hold to the one and despise the other. Ye cannot serve God and mammon." (Luke 16: 13). Private property is the more key concept because the creation of private property which allows for the accumulation of capital produces inequality and class conflict.

Jesus of the Gospels was an idealist and dreamer like many

before and after him. His was a magnanimous fantastic dream. Jesus believed that love (1 Corinthians 13), could bring equality and thus peace and the end of suffering for all humankind, suffering that had plagued humankind since early times. Jesus believed that if one truly loved his neighbor as much as he loved himself, equality would result and all the evils that inequality produces would disappear. Jesus knew also that this unconditional love of thy neighbor would have to be actively pursued by being translated into concrete everyday behavior.

Jesus's last command to "Love one another as I have loved you," what has been called 'the commandment of commandments' and is a statement of unconditional love, was considered the ultimate challenge in his message. As Henry Drummond in 'The Greatest Thing in the World' states: "Love understood by all, will be pouring forth its unconscious eloquence. It is the man who is the missionary, it is not his words. His character is his message." Thus, Jesus relates loving thy neighbor to his father's will and tells us that praying (alone) is not enough, that we must "do." For example, Matthew 79: 21 tells us "Not every one that saith unto me, Lord, Lord (prays), shall enter into the Kingdom of Heaven: but he that 'doeth' ("doeth" is intensely active) the will of my father which is in heaven." "Doeth" says that action must be taken.

As Drummond points out: "Thy will be done is intensely active." Nothing that Jesus teaches us is passive, which is understandable coming from an impassioned revolutionary and for who was, in fact, by word and deed, the world's first communist. Jesus in fact, lived a life and taught a philosophy of what could only be described as communistic. Throughout history this has been implicitly, if not explicitly, understood by many Christians. Christians, who following 1 John 2.6, "He that saith he abideth in him ought himself also so to walk, even as he walked," attempted to follow Jesus by living communal lives as based on the life and teachings of Jesus Christ and the scriptures. For example, Acts 3.43 through 45, "And fear came upon every soul: and many wonders and signs were done by the apostles. And all that believed were together and had all things common; and sold their possession and goods, and parted them to all men, as every man had need."

America's radical individualism is the exact opposite of communality, congregation, community, etc. It is the breeding ground for pleasure seeking self-love and pathological greed. Selfishness and self-centeredness. The hoarding of wealth is an emotional dysfunction. All the hoarding of wealth does is replace thumb sucking and security blankets for the emotionally insecure. The immature two-year old who has replaced hanging on to his mother's skirts with hanging on to "things." What is interesting is that whenever a group of devout Christians tried to follow Christ's example, the majority of so-called, self-proclaimed Christians, were usually the first to attack them vehemently and viciously. Christians would respond to their own brethren by destroying their property, burning their homes, beating and even killing them for nothing more than trying to live as Christ did.

Why? Because the 'far religious right' does not believe in the teachings of Jesus Christ! In fact, they dislike his teachings and reflect that hate of what Christ taught toward any group, even of their brethren, who would dare actually try to live their lives accordingly. Those who would follow Christ's communistic teachings, people who believe that living a communal life as in the motto of the 'three musketeers' "all for one and one for all" is the morally superior way to live, are most consistently seen by the 'far religious right' in a very negative light. The "far religious right" loudly proclaim and give lip service to Jesus Christ and Christianity only as a mask to hide their pure ugliness. It is a shield they hide behind and a source of being able to feel self-righteous and holier (better) than thou. To convince themselves that they have been "saved" and thus, have conquered their own mortality.

Phony, pseudo-Christian Fundamentalists, do not like to be exposed as trying to hide behind Christianity. They are numerous. They only give lip service to Jesus Christ and Christianity and use it as a tool to hide and excuse their un-Christian way of life. They use it to help alleviate what little conscience they have. They are very consistent in their hateful responses to unconventional groups like, for example, the Hutterites, people who are not only non-violent but non-threatening, non-imposing and who even try to isolate themselves so as not to bother anyone. Look, for example, at the 1960's so-called "hippies." They were primarily kids, and what was their core, basic primary message? It was simple, straightforward and very Christlike. It was, 'love thy neighbor as yourself'. Oh my God! What horror! What was as the response received from America's so-called Christians? "Satan is taking over our children." "They are a bunch of "commies." Jesus probably will not come back just to be imprisoned.

Yes, Jesus Christ's incredible dream was to bring about a communist (communal, congregational) society right here on earth and it was to be called "The Kingdom of God." The only attempt at true communism or communal life has been almost exclusively on the part of various Christian groups. The early pilgrims to America established communal villages, the Onieda community, Hutterites, Amish, Mennonites and so on. What most Americans recognize as a "communist" country, Marx himself would not. In fact, Marx was so (deliberately) misinterpreted during his own lifetime, that he said once, when looking at what people said was "Marxism," "One thing that I am not for sure and that is a Marxist." Marx's "modern communism" (the last stage of major development for societies) would be little different from the society which Jesus attempted to create right here on earth. As Donner acknowledged: "Unfortunately the Marxist vision is one thousand percent different from the Soviet Communist reality."

As Drummond discusses: "His (Jesus) immediate work was to enlist men in his enterprises, to rally them into a great company or society for the carrying out of his plans. The name by which this society was known was the Kingdom of God. Christ did not coin this name; it was an old expression, and good men had always hoped and prayed that some such society would be born in their midst. But it was never either defined or set a-going in earnest until Christ made its realization the passion of his life." Thus, Jesus Christ can be considered as the world's first 'communist.' "Hundreds of years before Christ's society was formed, its program had been issued to the world. I cannot think of any scene in history more dramatic than when Jesus entered the Church in Nazareth and read it to the people." What Drummond was referring to is Jesus's reading of Isaiah. Jesus wanted to create in effect, a communist society to carry out his father's will.

While Jesus believed that love could bring this kind of society about, Marx believed that because the rich would oppose it, just as the Roman Empire did, it would take an armed revolution to overthrow the established order controlled by them. Marx said that people were oppressed and held in check by their own religious beliefs. They believed that Caesar was a 'God.' Marx, like Jesus, attacked establishment religion. Marx recognized the control that the rich were wielding in institutionalized religion during his time. The rich used religion to keep the exploited and oppressed workers in their place and to prevent them from revolting. The way this was done was to use their own beliefs against them as a tool of control.

Marx pointed out that everything and anything contained in the scriptures that had to do even remotely with the "afterlife" was heavily emphasized and focused on. Attention was constantly focused away from the here and now. Attention was constantly focused away from concrete everyday life. Thus, through establishment religion, the rich could convince the worker that he should not be concerned with his plight here on earth no matter how austere or impoverished or how much of a struggle, because his real rewards come in the "afterlife." This allowed them to oppress and squeeze the worker for more and more. The establishment church ignored Isaiah 58: 3-7, in which employers were admonished for oppressing their workers. In this way, the worker would not question his own exploitation by the rich and would tend to simply accept his plight and things the way they were no matter how dehumanizing.

This is also one of the reasons why Jesus himself attacked establishment religion. It was a tool of control by the rich and powerful. The importance placed by Judeo-Christian teachings upon individual life and the endurance of suffering was capitalized on heavily. Augustine held that life and it's suffering were divinely ordained by God and must be borne accordingly. As the writings of the new testament assumed canonical form, suffering was reserved for Christians as something in which they could rejoice for two reasons: (1) God used suffering as a means of producing spiritual maturity; and (2) The very fact that Christians endured suffering was proof that they were children of God. So, the Christian was to worship a deity that demanded they live in perpetual fear and suffering.

Christians were to engage in an active, direct ministry of consolation and encouragement of their fellow sufferers. The relief to be provided was not removal of the suffering but a consolation that transformed the suffering into a positive force in the person's life. Capitalists could not find or even create a better more powerful philosophy to support and bolster their quest for riches and wealth at the expense of everyone else and they leaned on it heavily. White Christian ministers preached it to the slaves in the South. Originally bolstering the denial of death, in the 21st Century America it also bolsters resistance to things like humane euthanasia. This is why throughout history, rich powerbrokers always aligned forces with the powerbrokers of religion.

It is interesting to compare Marx and Jesus Christ. When Marx told General Weidemeyer that the ideas he expressed came from "others before him," he was not being humble. Marx certainly knew the scriptures. Marx was a Jew and his daughter, Laura who stayed with her father until his death, was a devout Lutheran. Compare, for example Acts 2: 44-45; "And all that believed were together and had all things in common; and sold their possessions, and goods, and parted them to all men as every man had need," with Marx's famous statement, in which he, like as did Jesus, deals with the age-old question of distribution of what society produces: "From each according to his capacity, to each according to his need." Unlike Jesus, Marx abhorred welfare because he recognized it as a dehumanizing form of social control. "From each according to his capacity" means that everyone is expected to contribute something.

Jesus, instead of seeing welfare as a form of social control, saw it as an act of compassion and love. Fundamentalist Christians hate welfare even more than Marx. So why do they not reject Christ as they do Marx? Because 'Christianity' provides them with a psychological tool to alleviate their conscience. They can give lip service to Christianity without having to actually do it. Also, Christ's teachings hold out the possibility, however slim (camel through the eye of a needle) for these money worshipping hate mongers, of forgiveness should all this stuff be really true. Also, off course, is the benefit of the psychological denial of death. Marx offers none of this. In fact, the majority of Christians no more accept Christ than they do Marx.

Jesus taught by actions more than words. In fact, what he said can only be fully understood in light of his concrete specific actions. His teachings were thematic and action oriented, focused on the here and now. The focus on the here and now is one of the single most important aspects of Christ's existence, for it provides us with the understanding of the nature of the link between our lives and 'The Kingdom of God.' As Burton Mack in his book 'Who wrote the New Testament?' states: "These teachings (Jesus's) are really a collection of pithy aphorisms that strike to the heart of ethical issues. A close analysis of these aphorisms reveals the intertwining of two themes that mark the genius of the (Jesus's) movement. One is a playful, heady challenge to take up a countercultural lifestyle." Jesus could be called the world's first hippie with his immense joy in and love of children and flowers, which he spoke more of than almost any other topic.

Mack goes on to state: "The other theme is an interest in the 'Kingdom of God.' The Kingdom of God referred to an ideal society, Jesus's dream, imagined as an alternative to the way in which the world was working under the Romans. But it also referred to an alternative way of life that anyone could take at any time. In this sense, the 'Kingdom of God' could be realized simply by daring to live differently from the normal conventions." "The kingdom of God in the teachings of Jesus was not an apocalyptic or heavenly projection of an otherworldly desire. It was driven by a desire to think that there must be a better way to live together than the present state of affairs, and it called for a change of behavior in the present on the part of individuals invested in the vision. Thus, the teachings of Jesus can be described as the creative combination of these two themes, or a challenge to the individual to explore an alternative social notion."

This is very crucial in understanding the notions of the 'second coming' and 'Thy kingdom come.' The most erroneous conception by Christians of Jesus's 'Kingdom of God' is that it is some heavenly distant realm in which someday they hope to 'go,' escape mortality. If his kingdom is 'coming', then they don't need to 'go'. There is nowhere to 'go', as the kingdom of God is in a sense, already 'here' and always has been. It just has not been realized. As John Crossan, in his book 'The historical Jesus, The Life of a Mediterranean Jewish Peasant,' discusses in 'A Kingdom of Here and Now' in that book, he quotes from Mark 13: 21-23, Mathew 24: 23-26 and Luke 17: 23 and other sources. "His disciples said to him; "When will the kingdom come," Jesus said, "It will not come by waiting for it" (This is why Jesus insisted upon, indeed, demanded action being taken by his followers.) "It will not be a matter of saying 'here it is' or 'there it is.'" (Gospel of Thomas 113).

Being asked by the Pharisees when the kingdom of God was coming he (Jesus) answered them: "Behold the kingdom of God is (is!) in the midst of you." (Luke 17: 20-21). Thus, the kingdom of God or 'heaven' is not in another world or 'out-there' in the 'heavens.' Instead, it is right here on earth. Also, heaven will only come about (for us) through our own actions! The responsibility for the coming of the kingdom, 'Thy kingdom come' is clearly laid at the feet of humankind! Crossan goes on to quote from the scriptures: "Jesus said, 'If those who lead you to say, 'see the kingdom in the sky', then the birds of the sky will precede you.' Rather, the kingdom is inside you, and it is outside of you." His disciples said to him, 'When will the New World come?' He said to them, 'What you look forward to has already come (already!) (Gospel of Thomas 3: 1, 51) and I say to you what you seek and inquire after beholding it is within you (within you!) (Dialogue of the Savior 16; Emmel et. al. 57).

Thus, heaven does not 'come', it is carried out. It is 'performed.' Jesus is telling us in the notion of the 'second coming,' that only if we act this prescribed way (as a Christian) will I then come. His second coming is not only contingent upon our actions, it is entailed in and brought about by our actions! This is our responsibility. We have to act to create 'The Kingdom of God' in our lives concretely, right here on earth in the here and now. When humanity does this, Jesus not only comes again, but so does the Kingdom of God. What does the Kingdom (heaven) entail? Certainly, if nothing else, it entails the society that Jesus advocated and called for in his declaration in the Temple of Nazareth and in his Sermon on the Mound; it was his dream.

It entails humankind caring for each other (the opposite of capitalism,) not for material existence. The Kingdom is where humanity does not live for himself at all, but for life itself, all life on earth. This is why we are told that: "The poor will inherit the earth." As Drummond put it: "He who cares not for the earth (material things) rules it for he cares not for it." To care about anything puts you in service to it. It is nobler to serve one's fellow man than to 'serve' inanimate objects. It is also why Jesus tell us: "Blessed are you the poor, for yours is (is!) the kingdom of heaven." It is heaven? Is? Jesus is telling us heaven is right here on earth, but it exists in the non-material life, the spiritual life, the intellectual life, the wise life.

We are told by the scriptures and Jesus to seek truth and wisdom. Wisdom and truth (knowledge) is referred to, almost countless times, throughout the scriptures and by Christ himself. "Wisdom is better than a strong man" (Book of Wisdom, 6:1.). Jesus's call for action was for action based on truth. It is interesting that America's founding fathers said that only an "enlightened" (knowledgeable) citizenry can maintain a free society, a notion totally lost on Fundamentalists. The Book of Wisdom also tells us: "For wisdom is more active than all active things; and reacheth everywhere by reason of purity (truth) 7: 24. We are told: "God loveth none but him that dwelleth with wisdom." 7: 28 and finally, "Therefore the desire of wisdom bringeth to the everlasting kingdom." 6:21.

The scriptures specifically address the requirement of thinking in Philippians 4:8; "Finally, brethren, whatsoever things are honest, whatsoever things are just, whatsoever things are pure, whatsoever things lovely, whatsoever things are of a good report; if there be any virtue, and if there be any praise, think on these things." Think! Think on these things! Not only are we required to think, but Philippians 4: 8 tells us some of the specific things we are supposed to think about! Heaven exists in the relationships among people "within and outside you." Jesus spent his life describing and demonstrating very specifically the behavior he was calling us to engage in, in the here and now! Thus, Jesus demonstrated, the purpose of all humankind is to serve others.

As Drummond points out: "The kingdom of God is a society that holds the worship of God to be mainly the service of humankind." To serve others is paramount to living a Christian life. As Colonel Donner's book argues: "To serve God is to serve man and to serve man is to serve God." As Jesus said: "Whatever you do unto these the least of mine, you do unto me." One could argue that like John said: "God is Love."; God is serving others. The specifics are found everywhere from the beginning of the scriptures to the description of the final judgement: "Giving the hungry food, the thirsty drink, befriending strangers, clothing the naked, visiting the sick and imprisoned." While Jesus commands us to serve others ('give'), Capitalism commands us to serve only ourselves (consume, 'take').

Capitalism, if anything, is the Anti-Christ. Although Fundamentalists are a good candidate for that designation. Capitalism makes the accumulation of more and more the paramount virtue and reality of human existence. Consumption is made holy, it is made sacred. Paul reminds us that to be content with having food and clothing is part of true happiness (1 Timothy 6: 7-8). Our individual selves, without any possessions or gifts are precious to God. No where in the scriptures are we told to bring goods or gifts to heaven. For what kind of society was Jesus calling? The same one that he said is the criteria to get into heaven (Matthew 25; 31-46).

Jesus, many times, referred to all of humanity as his brothers and tells us that God is "inside as well as outside us" (in the presence of others.) In effect, Jesus is telling us that we too are sons and daughters of God. We are told throughout the scriptures that we are God's "children." Jesus tells us very specifically, even repeating himself, what we have to do and be to enter heaven or a godly 'state' or 'existence.' The implication is that we can do that, and what a legacy to hand down to our descendants! Heaven has already been made for them right here on earth! It is a heaven made in the actions of people, Jesus's dream and goal come true!

This, however as Jesus spent his life emphasizing, requires actions, actions, actions. It requires perpetual doing. It requires us to simply act as he did. Jesus challenges us with his dream.

He challenges us to go after it. Fear enjoys a dominant and pervasive presence in our culture. Fear surrounds us; fear of death, fear of judgement, fear that the other guy has more than we do, fear of our own power. Fundamentalists have chosen a chaotic and fear ridden life and want to force it on the rest of us. Anita Moorjani ('What if this is Heaven?') argues that humans can release their fears and open their eyes to the reality of a heaven on earth. Jesus did not just call for action. As a role model, he taught action. Do not do as I say, do as I do. The necessity for people to be relentlessly active in their own destiny is paramount if they want to have any input at all into what happens to them. As Saul Alinsky in 'Rules for Radicals' argues: "The weakness as well as the strength of the democratic ideal has been the people." People cannot be free unless they are willing to sacrifice some of their interests to guarantee the freedom of others (one of the most consistent things that Jesus asked of us was to sacrifice for others). The price of democracy and freedom is the on-going pursuit (enshrined in the words "eternal vigilance" by the founding fathers) of the common good by all of the people." Alinsky goes on to point out: "One hundred and thirty-five years ago Tocqueville gravely warned that unless individual citizens were regularly involved in the action of governing themselves, self-government would pass from the scene."

Jesus's admonitions were focused on all of life i.e. the political, economic, social and so on. This is what is so important about Christ's teachings. They cover all human endeavors as a whole and tie them together. So is his challenge. The world's first real revolutionary, egalitarian, communist, visionary, indeed, citizen of the kingdom of God invites us. What an invitation! We can bring about the second coming through our own actions! Jesus never left! He is still here as he tried to tell us when he said: "Whenever two or more of you gather in my name, there I will be." Will be! Nothing less than an invitation, a challenge from the world's greatest revolutionary to raise 'hell' and, thus in the process heaven and he will be right there with us!

The author can think of no better start than to put stringent, legal limits on the accumulation of wealth. In fact, all else depends on it. Jesus expects us to act, indeed, commands us to act! Again, he warns us in Rev. 22: 12, "Behold, I am coming soon bringing my recompense, to repay every one for what he has done." "Done," not given lip service to! Jesus's final command to his disciples was "Love one another as I have loved you." This is the foundation, the rock, upon which his dream would be based. Jesus's dream is straight forward and simple. Humans living a communal existence as one. Jesus's dream for humankind was a communist society based on his final command. Like Marx, he would say no formal government was needed. And according to The Gospel of John, no damned church is needed either! ('The City Without a Church', Henry Drummond).

"Heaven" can only exist on the foundation of unconditional love (1 Corinthians; 13). To reiterate: Paul said: "Love is the fulfillment of the law", and Jesus stated: "Love is above all law," while Peter states: "above all things (above ALL things!) have fervent love among yourselves," but it was John who put it in a "nutshell"; "God is love" (IS!). Jesus's bottom line message is that heaven in the concrete here and now can only be constructed by humanity itself. The responsibility is ours. According to Jesus, the reality that "God is love" can only exist in relationships. The 'trinity' for example, is the revelation of the nature of God as community, as relationship itself.

Christ is a set of relationships inside of which we can live with integrity and in peace. Paul's metaphor for this living is "The body of Christ" (1 Corinthians; 12:13). There is no other ground for the Christian life except a common one. Christ is a living relationship among people, through concrete bonds of union in which we create Christ and ourselves. Becoming who we really are is a matter of learning how to become more and more connected. Trust is important. Without trust, there can be no sincere connection. Because ego can get in the way of trust, only the

76

dysfunctional psyche and personality lacks in and cannot trust.

During Paul's lifetime, the Christian church was a living organism communicated through relationships. Living in community means living in such a way that others can access me and influence my life. It means that I can get out of myself, "be ego free" and serve the lives of others. Community is a network of relationships. "Church," "Community," and "Union," is not just spiritual poetry. Paul writes that it is precisely "in your togetherness that you ARE Christ's body" (1 Corinthians; 12:27). It is a magnificently enlightening web of relationships which comprise an earth moving state of love in which we experience "salvation." In order to live and thus experience a Christian life, we must fully comprehend, be fully conscience of the fact that we are, in the same "boat".

Americans have neither accepted unity nor diversity very well at all, despite the fact that our currency, has the proclamation of intent of the new nation: "E Pluribus Unum," "From Many One." It was the intent of the founding fathers to move toward connectedness and relationships, while also honoring diversity. Connections with family and friends, people of different races, economic classes, gender, and personal orientations that are different than our own, and with animals and nature. This full connectedness, based on "Love is God," is essential to our "being." Without connectedness and communion, we can not exist fully, if at all, as our truest selves.

The "saved" individual is a product of a bonding process in community, marriage, families, nations, institutions, organizations. Dr. Martin Luther King Jr. saw clearly, that we face a real choice in our relations between chaos and community. America needs the moral revival Jesus attempted to spark in his day, a revival to bring about beloved community. Jesus fully understood that what we do unto others, we really do to ourselves. Jesus, of course warned: "What so ever you do unto these the least of mine, you do unto me." One of the main obstacles to beloved community continues to be the fear, of what- ever genre, that people in power have used for centuries to divide and conquer God's children. We are, whatever our differences, all in the same "boat." Reverend Dr. William Barber (In foreword to; 'Reconstruction of the Gospel: Finding Freedom from Slaveholder Religion').

Jesus's vision of "church" is simple: "Two or three gathered in my name" (Matthew; 18:20). "and I am with you." This is why Jesus sends the disciples out "two by two" (Mark; 6:7). "Church" is community, even a community of two. It is both method and message. "May they all be one, so the world may believe it was you who sent me, that they may be one as we are one, with me in them and you in me" (John; 17:21, 23). "The Christian's inner self is inseparable from all the other "I's" who live in Christ, so that they all form one" ('The Inner Experience: Notes on Contemplation; Thomas Merton). Early Christians hoped for a different future, a different society, a different life. For Jesus, 'church' was an 'alternative lifestyle' ('The Church is Supposed to be an Alternative Lifestyle', Rohr., 'What if this is Heaven', Moorjani).

They hoped for a transition to a society less fearful, oppressive, destructive, more peaceful. This hope was embedded in Christ's teachings and in the Christian ethic of resistance, and hope calls on Jesus's followers, "his church," to live as not just a contrast but as a contradictory community in rejection of society of the times ('Transition Movement for Churches', Timothy Gorringe and Rose Beckham). This was Paul's missionary strategy. Jesus's followers, his "church," practiced sharing abundance and living in simplicity. The dream was for humankind sharing resources, living simply, and creating a sustainable and non-violent future.

In the Christian life "there are no more distinctions between Jew and Greek, slave and free, male and female, but all of you are one in Christ" (Galatians: 3:28.) This is not just a religious idea but a socioeconomic message. For Jesus, forgiving, healing, social and economic justice are the only real evidence of a shared life. Peacemaking, forgiveness, and reconciliation is the signature of heaven in the here and now ('Essential Teachings on Love', Richard Rohr). God is exchanges of mutual knowing and loving, and perfect giving and perfect receiving is reality as communion. "Perfect" as stated here is being a pure act of love. It is the arc of the moral universe. Jesus's efforts were directed toward bending that arc. "The arc of the moral universe is long, but it bends toward justice" ('A Testament of Hope: The Essential Writings and Speeches of Martin Luther King, Jr.', James W. Washington, Ed.).

Part Three

A Dream Gone Awry

Historians have argued that the closest to Marx's "modern communism" that any group has ever come were the "communes" of early colonial America, both religious and secular. A hallmark of Marx's "modern communism" is the utter absence of any type of formal, bureaucratic government, that is, legalistic government based on written laws. Marx in describing "modern communism" stated: "And government as we know it will wither away." "As we know it" has been argued to be any form or type of 'formal' bureaucratic government. Thus, any regulative or governing entity would harken back to and be much closer to those of Marx's "primitive communism," such as tribal councils, village elders, etc. Thus, it has been argued that the closest any group has come to that is the relatively isolated communes of early colonial America. Some would include Native American Tribes at that time.

Other concepts of human living arrangements in colonial America also included some aspects of 'communal' living. 'Communes' have also been referred to as 'utopian communities' or 'utopian socialists,' etc. Communal living obviously entails the generic notion of 'socialism' which goes back to earliest humankind, hunting and gathering tribes as a moral dilemma. Old Alley Oop was one of the best hunters in the tribe. One day old 'Oop' got trampled by a huge wildebeest (oops!) and both legs were totally crushed. It was obvious that he would never hunt again. What could he have contributed to the survival of the tribe? Humans are gregarious animals; they live, work, produce, consume and play in groups. They are 'social' creatures.

'Social' refers to the group itself as a reality and the relations between people who make up the group. 'Social' is related to 'individual' in the context of the 'individual' being a member of the group and participating in the 'group', the relations between people in the group and to the group. One notion associated with this is what is good for the group is good for me, because I am part of the group and vice-versa. Old 'Oop' presented a 'social' dilemma for the group. What could they do? What were their options?

There are three: 1). They could just walk off and leave ol' Oop to die. 2). They could club Oop in the head to relieve him of his pain. 3). They could take Oop back to the tribe for care. Fundamentalists today, without even giving it a thought, would take option one.

This brings the question to the group, what is their responsibility? Even primitive humans had the capacity to empathize with and feel compassion for his fellow humans. Taking Oop back to the tribe to be taken care of was an act of responsibility. It was a 'social' or 'socialist' act, a primarily moral act, not a political one. A 'socialist' act or 'socialism' through time comes to be as much as, if not more so, a political act as a moral act as formal governments arose and became involved in the decisions and methods to handle it when such a situation as Oops arose. Entailed in this is the perceived range of situations the 'responsibility' of the group to the individual covers, and it is always intertwined with what is seen or not seen as moral.

Is making sure that everyone (which includes me) has the food, clothing, shelter and medical care necessary for survival the equivalent of taking old Oop back to the tribe? The moral foundations for socialist acts go far back in history. For example, Jesus warned: "What so ever you do unto these the least of mine, you do unto me!" The most significant part that the rise of formal government has influenced is the method by which that group responsibility is carried out. Thus, 'Socialism' is more a method of than a type or form of government. The U.S. has had major aspects of socialism since it's founding. Public schools, libraries, police departments, fire departments, the military, farmers coops, are all pure socialism. The essence of 'socialism' entails resources being pooled or collected from the whole group to provide for necessities that the individuals who make up the group could not provide for themselves.

Yet, the U.S. is not considered a 'socialist' country, despite the fact that much of it is and always has been. Some argue that socialism is 'forced,' not voluntary thus, the U.S. is not socialist. Well, just try not paying your taxes! There is a reason why taxes are not voluntary. If I get fire services whether I pay my taxes or not, why would I pay them? It would not be in my own personal, individual interests to pay them. To hell with everybody else, I'll keep my money in my pocket and let them provide me with fire services, if I need them. It is called selfishness and greed.

Christianity is a religion of unity. 'Church,' which in Jesus's native tongue had the same meaning as the English word 'following,' has a different connotation today. 'Church' today is generally taken to mean 'community' as in a 'community of followers.' Christianity is socialistic. As American colonists (at least the second wave of pilgrims) sought religious freedom, the unanticipated consequences ended up being an atmosphere of much religious diversity. Along with numerous denominations, churches, sects and cults, all kinds of fringe religious communes were also present in colonial America, which created not unity but conflict between and even within groups.

The main reason for the insistence upon the separation of church and state by the founding fathers was to protect Christians from Christians, who upon occasion would hang, burn to death, or stone each other to death for things like witchcraft or blasphemy. Christians seemed to be the only ones dumb enough to believe in witches. This explains James Madison's statement: "The purpose of separation of church and state is to keep forever from these shores the ceaseless strife that has soaked the soil of Europe in blood for centuries."

One colonial fringe commune was the women of the wilderness commune. They combined pagan, Christian, and Jewish traditions in their own religion. In early colonial America these communes were commonly lead by charismatic leaders with exalted religious or moral and ethical ideals, the most common being religious. These communes expressed a wide variety and mixture of different models of governance or regulation, marriage, labor, wealth, etc. Hundreds of these communal arrangements were scattered around the American landscape, from the time of the earliest pilgrims.

In this sense, it is accurate to say that America was founded by these 'communal' groups as much as by those seeking wealth in the new world, i.e. the first wave of 'pilgrims' to the colonies (The majority on the Mayflower were not 'pilgrims', they were still loyal to the church of England). As discussed by Kurt Andersen in 'Fantasyland: How America Went Haywire A 500-Year History,' the first wave of 'pilgrims' to the colonies did not come seeking religious freedom, they came out of greed, seeking riches and wealth. It was the second wave of pilgrims who came seeking religious freedom.

All in all, the early colonial years were out and out barbaric ('The Barbarous Years', Bernard Bailyn.) As related by Bailyn: "For the Puritans war with the natives was a struggle with satanic forces and whose "extirpation" was a Christian duty." "The bloody massacre in Virginia of 1622, looting and destroying by fire the Indians crops in the fields and in storage, were still in progress when elsewhere, the Puritans small but efficient army, burned alive the hundreds of unsuspecting Pequot men, women and children. They slaughtered all those they found attempting to escape, then hunted the rest down as they fled." He also says, "gestures that the English took as signs of submission and of the legitimacy of their conquest, dismembered body parts, heads, hands, scalps, and torn-off strips of skin, had become commonplace objects among such gently people as the pilgrims."

The attitude of early colonial Christians toward America's native population was clearly expressed in that noted Christian Pilgrim, Miles Standish's actions. As discussed by Bailyn: "the pressure on the natives had reached the point of brutality. In retaliation, the indians began planning an assault. When word was received of a pending conspiracy at Wessagusset, Standish and a small troop were sent off to repeal the attack before it began." "They did their work quickly and savagely. They lured the leading warriors into the blockhouse and then stabbed them to death one after another." He also says, "the youngster who accompanied the warriors, Standish 'caused to be hanged.' Then, Standish cut off the head of the "bloody and bold villain," believed to have inspired the conspiracy and brought it back to Plymouth in triumph, where it was displayed on the blockhouse together with a flag made of a cloth soaked in the victim's blood." And that "Standish was received 'with joy' but not to universal acclaim."

One of the earliest, historically significant American colonies was Plymouth colony. It was founded in 1620 in what is now known as Plymouth, Massachusetts. The colony had written into its charter a system of communal property and labor. Plymouth colony, like many others, reflected a collectivist impulse in various offshoots of Protestant Christianity, with names like the "True Levelers" and the "Diggers." The Romans would have at least considered Jesus as a 'leveler.' Mass movements of groups, usually religious, who believed that property and income distribution should be community oriented, and for the good of the whole group. This pragmatic philosophy was common in the 1600's, which is why the Plymouth colonists settled for a charter which did not create a legalistic private property system as we know it today.

It can be argued that the religious communes of early Colonial America, harkening back to 1st Century Christianity and Acts 3.43-45, were an attempt to realize Jesus's dream. Jesus thought his dream could be realized through the hearts of all people. So, what went awry? Greed? Marx thought so and, thus, argued the only way that kind of society can come about is through armed revolution. Both Jesus and Marx so far in history, have proved to be wrong, neither the hearts of people or revolution, has brought about Jesus's dream. So how did Jesus's dream go awry in America? The early years of the colo-

86

nial era were marked by irregular religious practices, minimal communication between remote settlers, a population of 'undesirables,' wide distances and poor transportation.

Regular religious practices were most common, to the degree there were any, in the isolated religious communes. As depicted by Bailyn in 'The Barbarous Years,' conditions in early colonial America were difficult to say the least. "They lived conflicted lives, beset with conflicts experienced, rumored, or recalled, unrelenting racial conflicts, ferocious and savage religious conflicts, as bitter within as between confessions." Bailyn continues, "social disagreements, personality conflicts, and theological controversies within emerged quickly." He also says, "the great migration consisted of a sprawl of small settlements scattered across the countryside and dominated by contentious magistrates and clerics of increasingly divergent views."

Bailyn relates; "The development of a society of divergent opinions and discordant modes of behavior, differences and antagonisms that would be resolved to the extent that they were resolved, at times by persuasion, at other times by intimidation, and at moments of crisis by vengeful brutality." Utopian settlements were attempted against his tumultuous background by religious groups such as the Mennonites, Shakers, Hutterites, Mormons and Moravians. Political and social ideas were adapted from such reformers as John Humphrey Noyes, founder of the Oneida Community (the reader may have Oneida 'silverware' in their kitchen drawers), as well as directly from the scriptures. However, religious diversity led to intolerance and conflict in a struggling land.

There was commonly a mixture of political alliances, economic differences, ethnic feuds and others. In conflicts, religious differences were common and consistent. Religion or religious beliefs were commonly the main cause of conflict. The conflicts increased or decreased with the warp and woof of economic development and historical events into the 20th century. By the

87

20th century, the doctrine of separation of church and state had suppressed much, if not most, conflicts between religious groups. However, at the beginning of the 20th century, there was increasing conflict between religious traditionalists or 'premillennialists' and modernists, who embraced science, facts, knowledge, learning, rational thought processes and progress.

It produced 'The Fundamentals: A Testimony to the Truth', 1914, consisting of a set of anti-modernist essays. The foreword described it as being published in the belief that the time had come where a new statement of the fundamentals of Christianity should be made ('The Fundamentals'.) The argument of the 'Fundamentals' was that modern science is a threat to religion. At their 1920 annual conference, Northern Baptists stated: "We view with increasing alarm the havoc which rationalism is working in our churches." They explicitly endorsed the irrational or 'magical thinking.' The editor or the Northern Baptist weekly, reflecting 'The Fundamentals' in an editorial, gave alarmed Christian fantasists a name; fundamentalism is a protest against rationalistic interpretations of Christianity, which seeks to discredit supernaturalism. This rationalism is robbing Christianity of it's supernatural content. When robbed of supernaturalism, it ceases to be a religion and becomes an exalted system of ethics. ('Fantasyland How America went Haywire, Kurt Andersen)

Fundamentalism is a fear of and rejection of fact-based, rational thinking. An essay by J.J. Reeve of Southwestern Baptist Theological Seminary, encapsulates the sentiment of the 'Fundamentals.' "In the array of scientific facts all religion would be evaporated." "This is the ideal of the evolutionary hypotheses. The rationalist would rejoice, but the Christian mind shrinks in horror from it." ('The Fundamentals; vol. 3, 'My Personal Experience with the Higher Criticism.' J.J. Reve) Reeve admits that he is closing his mind to expanding knowledge. He expresses fear, even horror at the thought of confrontation with science.

Fundamentalism became a growing phenomenon within Christianity. ('Dominionism Rising: A Theocratic Movement Hiding in Plain Sight', Frederick Clarkson) Fundamentalism is obsessed with biblical supremacy, literalism and exclusion (an us-them, dualistic mentality). The egoic need for clarity and certitude leads fundamentalists to use the scriptures in a legalistic, literal, mechanical, closed-ended (and closed minded) and very authoritarian way. The ego rarely, if ever, asks real questions and mostly gives quick answers. This invariably leaves ego driven, fundamentalist minds and groups utterly trapped in their own cultural moment in history. There is an especially telling passage in Mark's Gospel where Jesus becomes angry with his disciples, who are unable to understand his clearly metaphorical language.

Jesus tells them to watch out for the "leaven" of the pharisees and the "leaven" of Herod. Taking him literally, they began looking quizzically at one another because they did not have any bread (Mark 8: 14-16). Is Herod Bread a new brand that they had not heard about? Jesus responded with frustration: "Do you think I am talking about bread? You're still not using your heads are you? You still don't get the point, do you? Though you have ears, you still don't hear; though you have eyes, you still don't see!" (Mark 8: 17-18) They do not yet know that the only way to talk about transcendental things is through metaphor. But early stage religious people are invariably literalists. Jesus consistently used stories, images, the language of the metaphor, simile, symbol and analogy to teach. This approach demands more of us, especially a thinking mind.

Fundamentalists consistently avoid this in favor of more mechanical readings that they can limit and control. Words are fingers pointing to the mountain, but words are never the mountain itself (MLK would agree). Not knowing this has kept much religion like Fundamentalism, infantile, arrogant, and dangerous." ('Jesus Plan for a New world: The Sermon on the Mount', Richard Rohr) Jesus rarely, if ever, taught by proffering theological statements of the kind in which organized churches have specialized for centuries. The Good Samaritan parable is a classic example of the way Jesus taught. The two who passed by the injured man on the road were following the law, i.e. that one defiled oneself if he touched a dead or dying man. The Samaritan put love above the law and rendered help to the man. The lesson is clear; fundamentalism in any form is wrong! "Love is above all law" Jesus said ('Stealing Jesus: How Fundamentalism Betrays Christianity', Bruce Bawer).

The core of the fundamentalist Christian belief is their acceptance of the inerrancy of the bible which is over 2,700 years old. The scriptures representing the word of God are taken literally and legalistically as a blueprint for and regulating behavior and relationships in the 21st century A.D. One of the fundamental elements of far-right Christians is a belief that the bible prophesies a second coming of Christ. The second coming would be signaled by "signs of the times" that foretell the second coming. There have been many "second comings" throughout history. The first anticipated event is the rapture, where in faithful Christians would be "caught up together to meet the Lord in the air." The rest of humanity will be left to endure the "tribulation," a series of horrible catastrophic events. The second coming of Christ, the battle of Armageddon, and the tribulation will be followed then by the millennium and final judgement. The righteous who will meet the Lord during the rapture, will avoid all of these calamities of terror. The reason for their salvation and selection for the rapture would be their unwavering, unquestioning, adherence to the prophecy and the scriptures. Christian Fundamentalists share common ground with the Jews. Their Christian fate and that of the entire planet is at stake. The Christian right is committed to supporting and protecting Israel at all cost. A major component of such support is U.S. financial aid to Israel together with political support and with arms. Also, they oppose any U.N. resolutions seen as detrimental to Israel, and they condone any Israeli actions. This involves compromising America's political ideals, process and parties in the name of a religion in another country, all out of fear. Ironically, it is all for self-interest, because the 'far religious right' could give a rat's pettootie less for the Jewish people. Their ultimate vision is the conversion of Jews.

The turn of the 21st century presented the shocking revelation of the depth to which Christian fundamentalists had penetrated leadership of the American Governing system at all levels, Federal and State. The underlying beliefs of our elected officials and the ways that U.S. policy has been and still is distorted by religious and un-American convictions, is a direct threat to our democratic form of government. It is a direct threat to freedom. Religious motivations, goals and their proponents have had a free-hand in shaping U.S. responses, with little if any regard for the long-term consequences. The 'Christian far right' began its political crusade with corporate and wall street backing in the 1950's and gained momentum and influence in the late 1980's and into the 21st century ('One Nation Under God', Kevin Kruse).

The 'far religious right' has been dedicated to electing candidates that share their conservative religious values, as symbolized by the core issues of abortion and less government. The common mantra for the religious right and wealthy libertarian elites, would be oligarchs, is that government is the enemy. In the U.S., Christian fundamentalists have focused on the ballot box. They are as much a political party as they are a religion. One result has been rapid escalation in support for Israel.

Christian Fundamentalists also resort to violence and terrorism. The U.S. invasion of Iraq, for example, was motivated by desires to protect Israeli interests in the Mid-East and to secure Israel as much as it was about oil. "I'm saddened that it is politically inconvenient to acknowledge what everyone knows: The Iraq war is largely about oil." ('The Age of Turbulence: Adventures in a New World', Alan Greenspan).

Fundamentalist interpretations of the life and teachings of Christ and the Scriptures are twisted and distorted to emphasize to their followers what they stand to gain rather than what they can give, like their service for, or sharing with others. Christian fundamentalists emphasize personal gain above the welfare of others, and a belief that this inherent selfishness and self-interest will be rewarded. Greed is one of the dominant motivators in their desire to bring about the "end times" because, according to scripture, that's when the wealth of the world will be given to the 'righteous' (them). They voted for Donald Trump because they believed that he would bring and end to the world ('Trump Will Start the End of the World: Claim Evangelicals Who Support Him', Cristina Maza).

The 'far religious right' also shares with wall street, the big banks, corporations and investors the notion that "greed is good." Evangelical Pastor, Joel Osteen for example, argues that Jesus "wants us to be rich." They think nothing of exploiting other people to advance selfish interests under the guise of religion and relentlessly attack with disgust and disdain those who Jesus called "the least of mine." About the nicest thing they say about Jesus's "least of mine" is that they are a bunch of no good, lazy, welfare cheats and bums. Children, handicapped, or the elderly have no meaning to them. They treat them like the grade school bully extorting lunch money from other kids.

James Mattil, the managing editor of Global Focus put it this way: "Most important is the belief that the divine word of any particular religion is the one and only truth, subject to no compromise." Hence fundamentalist Christians know, without doubt, that when the Armageddon arrives, true Christian believers will be saved, and non-Christians condemned. It is not good enough in their mind that they are going to be 'saved' but they must believe that others are not. This belief is aggressive and vicious. The problem is that for fundamentalists, eternal salvation requires more than leading a certain kind of life, it demands certain achievements during one's life, conquering land, taking power over governments and all social aspects of life, converting non-believers or destroying the non-converted. They would be a role model of brutality and barbarism for ISIS, if they ever took complete control of government.

Christian fundamentalists resort to violence and use the bible to justify an oppressive ideology. There is a large overlap among the hundreds of militia type groups in the U.S., White supremacists, nationalists, and Christian identity believers. Militia groups, the KKK, and other far right radical groups in the U.S. overlap and identify with fundamentalist Christianity and each other, which connects the religious right with radical libertarian ideology of wealthy elites. They are ultra-conservative to say the least ('The Fundamentals of Extremism: The Christian Right in America', Kimberly Baker. 'Bring the War Home; The White Power Movement and Paramilitary America', Kathleen Belew).

As discussed by Ashtari ('KKK Leader Disputes Hate Group Label; We're A Christian Organization', Shadee Ashtari), "The leader of the Traditionalist American Knights of the Ku Klux Klan, argues that the group is a non-violent Christian organization." "We're a Christian organization Frank Ancona, the groups Imperial Wizard, told Virginia's NBC 12." The Ku Klux Klan is composed entirely of white, Anglo-Saxon Christian American citizens, who believe that their race and religion are superior to those of people of other colors and religions. The KKK uses scripture and teachings from Christian pastors to support its cause and justify its actions. They are fundamentalists through and through.

These American Christian white supremacists believe that all non-white people are inferior and that they have no place in the United States which is only a home for white Christians. All members of the KKK must be one hundred percent white and Christian. Klansmen feel a strong sense of hate toward anyone who is not of their race and religion. They discriminate against and use acts of violence to intimidate and hold down other races. One of their hallmark symbols is the "light of God," the burning cross. The number one source, and sometimes the only source, of knowledge for the KKK is the bible. Members of the Klan, like other fundamentalists with which they readily and regularly intermix and associate with, go to the same churches and believe in the literal inerrancy and truth of the bible. Throughout history, many Klansmen and leaders were ordained ministers.

Legislation and the creation of "hate crimes" and their prosecution, along with other developments, reduced the membership, activities and influence of the KKK in the U.S. going into the 21st century. However, the Ku Klux Klan underwent a significant revival, as witnessed by events like their participation in the white nationalist "Unite the Right" rally in Charlottesville. This was more effective than when a preacher used Christianity to revive and incite the Ku Klux Klan. "On Oct. 16, 1915, Fundamentalist Methodist preacher William Joseph Simmons and at least 15 other men climbed Stone Mountain in Georgia. They built an altar, set fire to a cross, took an oath of allegiance to the "Invisible Empire" and announced the revival of the Ku Klux Klan." "Beneath a makeshift altar glowing in the flickering flames of the burning cross, they laid a U.S. flag, a sword and a Holy Bible." "The angels that have anxiously watched the reformation from its beginnings," said Simmons, who declared himself Imperial Wizard, "must have hovered about Stone Mountain and shouted hosannas to the highest heavens." "The Klan dismantled by President Ulysses S. Grant was "born again" that night in 1915 on Stone Mountain, and Christianity was used to justify a second wave of terror." ('The preacher who used Christianity to revive the Ku Klux Klan', DeNeen L. Brown)

By 1980, religious fundamentalists used very similar rhetoric about Christian Supremacy as the Klan. The 'far religious right' and the Klan have grown closer together almost as one. The Reverend Bailey Smith, the President of the Southern Baptist Convention, announced in 1980 that: "God almighty does not hear the prayer of a Jew." The Klan takes direct action against those who do not share its beliefs or those who it simply views as inferior based on its reading of the bible. Klansmen recognize the difference of other groups and translate them into justification for hate ('Behind the Mask of Chivalry', Nancy MacLean, 'The Ku Klux Klan: An Encyclopedia', Michael Newton, 'The Fiery Cross', Wade, Wyn Craig). It can be argued that in a real sense, the 'far religious right' has become the "anti-Christ." Jesus taught nonviolence (Matthew 5: 38 -48), and he never instructed that his gospel be spread coercively; rather, he tells his disciples that if they were not willingly received in a city, they should shake the dust off their feet and go to the next city (Mark 6: 11). The new testament further instructs Christians to be law abiding, exemplary citizens of the state (Rom. 13: 1-8; 1 pet. 2: 13-30). This is in direct contradiction to the fundamentalists who are working to destroy freedom of religion in the U.S., by creating a Christian theocracy in America and by replacing its civil law system and indeed, the constitution with the bible ('Dominionism Rising', Clarkson). The 'far religious right' becomes more and more aggressive every year.

Parallel, and in conjunction with the rise of the religious right, was the movement by wealthy ultra-conservatives, libertarians, would be oligarchs, to reverse FDR's new deal. It would not only take control of government but would literally buy most of it off through privatization of all government functions and services, except maintaining a military defense system ('Democracy in Chains', Nancy MacLean). This is being accomplished by an alliance, an alliance of common interests between the rich and the 'far religious right' who have the same common enemy, Democratic government. The rich want a corporate oligarchy and the 'far religious right' want a theocracy. They have intertwined, blended together and are completely compatible for one thing, turning Jesus into a capitalist.

Rich, would-be oligarchs realized that money alone could not achieve their goals; they had to own, control legislatures. They needed a powerful force, an army of 'boots on the ground,' useful idiots. They realized that this could be accomplished by throwing a yoke around Jesus's neck and harness him in the service of their interests and needs. That is exactly what they did ('One Nation Under God' Kevin Kruse). Along with an army of 'boots on the ground;' who also comprise a large and devoted voter base, 'far right libertarian,' would-be oligarchs, primarily the Koch brothers and their cabal of fellow wealthy ultra-conservatives, constructed an immense political system, machine, which rivals the G.O.P. itself. In effect, the G.O.P. (Greed Over People) is now merely an arm of what Charles Koch has dubbed as the "Kochtopus" ('Dark Money', Jane Mayer).

Starting then in the beginning of the 20th century, there were two significant movements that have largely determined the history of the U.S. since. They were 1) the Fundamentalist 'far religious right' movement to take control of government and 2) the movement of the rich to take control of government. The two movements merged to create the greatest threat to freedom and democracy in America today. The founding fathers feared and recognized the dangers of both. The rise of industrial capitalism in the 19th century, the big banks, and corporate monopolies brought widespread deplorable conditions and human suffering, from the continuation of slavery, to child labor, sweat-shop conditions, and "Robber Barons." These conditions set the stage for Franklin D. Roosevelt's 'New Deal.'

President Roosevelt, a devout and practicing Episcopalian, found these conditions to be morally unacceptable and deplorable. Roosevelt's 'New Deal' in particular, the breaking up of the big banks that threatened our democracy, was designed to remedy these ills and maladies of our country with it's run away capitalist system. Roosevelt shared the founding fathers view that corporations and the rich are a direct threat to democracy. Almost immediately, the rich and investors, bankers, wall street and corporate America revolted and set out to destroy and reverse Roosevelt's 'New Deal.' This goal evolved into destroying Democratic government itself and replacing it with a corporate oligarchy.

Corporate America waged war on the 'New Deal' and any government interference, in their quest for the amassing of more wealth. They quickly realized the need for 'boots on the ground' and recognized the potential power of harnessing to their wagon, conservative Christian America. Corporations used clergymen early on in their PR war against Roosevelt's 'New Deal,' which gave the working person things like social security. Corporate America used the strategy of using Jesus to achieve their personal interests. The starting point was to define and create America as a "Christian" nation, a direct contradiction of the intent of the founding fathers. "The government of the United States is not, in any sense, founded on the Christian religion." (1797 treaty of Tripoli, signed by President John Adams and unanimously ratified by the U.S. Senate)

In their 'make America a Christian nation' campaign, corporate America used simple minded ornamental mottos like "under God" and "In God we trust," which became parts of a clever business plan. Wall street interests created a marketing machine behind American godliness. Their agenda included the pledge of allegiance, "One nation under God," and other foundations of American patriotism. It was a crass play on patriotism, emotions and ignorance. An un-holy alliance of greedy businessmen, venal clergy and self-serving conservative politicians exploited shamelessly American spirituality and patriotism for personal and partisan gain. ('One Nation Under God', Kruse) A "Christian" America was not the intent of the nation's founders; it was the deliberate invention of and the irony of corporate creation and involvement in the 'Christian America' campaign and movement.

The relationship between church and state went through a

profound transformation in the 1950's. Since then, the history of religion in the U.S. has been largely also a history of capitalism. Business opponents of Roosevelt's 'New Deal' joined forces with crusading ministers to place religious piety at the core of American society. The claim that the U.S. was founded and then flourished as a Christian nation is an all-American falsehood and fraud, disseminated in the 1950's through today by a combination of reactionary businessmen, political leaders, religious fanatics and dupes, often one and the same. The founding documents of the United States; The Federalist Papers, Articles of Confederation, and the Constitution, use the words Jesus Christ, Christianity, or God, zero times. Those words do not appear one single time in any of the founding documents. Also, the Constitution specifically prohibits "religious tests" for public office. America had become a fantasyland. Anything that deals mainly in fantasies rather than realities, and programs based on them create an artificial and unreal plan for an imaginary future which cannot help us understand or find solutions to the crisis of modern times. One of the most toxic mixes in recent decades entails the parallel developments of deliberate, well-funded "Fake News" and the rise of well-funded fundamentalism. Feeding off of and inflaming each other, they created a very toxic and dangerous mix. Fox News and radio talk shows for decades built an audience largely on "Fake News." Research of people who predominantly watch only one source of news has time and again shown that Fox News viewers are both less informed and the most misinformed of all groups.

The format for Fox News was not primarily to give the news, but to tell people what they wanted to hear, and play on all their prejudices, biases, etc. This is done by telling people that only Fox News tells you what is true, literally no other source does. This created a dependency on Fox News as a source of security for insecure people in what they think and believe. It created a spiral into which people were sucked into the fantasy world of Fox news. In this way, Rupert Murdoch and Roger Ailes set the stage by building an audience for a would-be authoritarian leader, a would-be dictator, and a fantasy reality to support him based on their "fake news." It is no coincidence that the demographics of Fox News viewers and that of Donald Trump's supporters are virtually identical.

Fox viewers and Trump supporters are predominantly white, older, more rural, less educated, working class, fundamentalists. Over 81% of fundamentalists voted for and/or support Donald Trump. Wealthy elites, using the G.O.P., aligned with the 'far religious right' for decades in an effort to build political power ('One Nation Under God', Kruse). The hate, meanness, ugliness of the G.O.P. and the religious right is no coincidence. The greed of Wall Street (where 'greed' is 'good') and the 'far religious right's "God" are quite compatible when it comes to the treatment of people who are not just like them. These are people who Jesus called "the least of mine." The 'far religious right,' defends capitalism as much as they defend their twisted religion. Like Trump, capitalism can do no wrong. Any figure who makes any critical comments about things, like predatory business practices is immediately attacked and vilified by the 'far religious right'. Any figure who calls for increased compassion for the poor and oppressed are immediately attacked and vilified by the 'far religious right.' Jesus Christ's entire life was spent on helping the poor and oppressed, attacking those of wealth and privilege and those who abuse the weak. It is amazing to see the vitriol and hatred pour forth from the 'far religious right' toward anyone who simply points out what Christ was all about. Well I'll be darn; Christianity should be about helping the poor.

The 'far Christian right,' in their twisted, tormented, sick minds, have taken the Jesus of the gospels, the good shepherd, who fed and healed the poor and overturned the money changers in the temple, and made him a poster child for wall street, the big banks, corporate investors and greed. America's entire myth is rooted in the idea of manifest destiny. This is the belief that God had chosen the pilgrims to subdue and colonize, no matter how barbaric their behaviors. ('The Barbarous Years', Bernard Bailyn) The idea of manifest destiny is still deeply embedded in the psyche of America. New myths were required to motivate the tremendous effort it took to build a new country out of forests, mountains, plains and deserts of this virgin land. The Calvinist movement with its focus on "salvation through hard work," and the idea that God put humans on earth for the sole purpose of working to further the glory of God at whatever he sets his hand to, provided exactly the kind of belief that could tie in with manifest destiny and build a new nation.

Calvinist doctrine also was central in transforming traditional capitalism into modern capitalism. ('The Protestant Ethic and the Spirit of Capitalism', Max Weber) From the very beginning, American Christians believed that commerce and conquest, no matter how vicious and brutal, were not only a practical necessity of survival, but also a divinely ordained mission. For believers in the American Dream, the creation of the nation itself was proof of God's divine favor toward the U.S. Today, that dream is failing and falling apart, more and more, for more and more of its citizens. For example, today, America is now the world's largest debtor, both as a nation and individually. (home mortgages, student and vehicle debt) Military adventurism and imperialist corporate America, fueled by the military industrial complex of which President Eisenhower warned us has weakened the U.S. both financially and morally, and it's influence in world affairs is losing ground to China, Russia and other emerging powers.

The fact that America is subject to the laws of history and economics on the world stage, just like every other country, violates its foundational myth. The 'far religious right' argues that the U.S. was born under manifest destiny. The idea of "American exceptionalism," that the rules of the world don't apply to us, is deeply embedded into the psyche of the nation. American exceptionalism was established by the fact that the fore-fathers, for the first time in history, took government away from Gods (Caesar, Roman Empire) and the control of Gods (Divine right of Kings, middle ages) and placed it exclusively in the hands of the citizenry.

The Declaration of Independence states: 'to secure these rights, Governments are instituted among MEN, deriving their just powers from the CONSENT OF THE GOVERNED." (not from God or anyone ordained by God) American exceptionalism is: "We the People." The fundamentalist myth has always been expressed in religious terms, that God supports America in a special way. When the nation struggles and falters with internal problems detrimental to it's population, it creates much cognitive dissonance on the part of true believers. With illogical and irrational gymnastics of all sorts, the answer invariably is some kind of "boogieman" causing it. Usually that "boogieman" is "socialism," or a lack of prayers on the part of people.

When fear keeps us out of touch with reality, it sets the stage for much cognitive dissonance, produced by the difference between what is real and what we think or believe is real. To solve the dissonance by rejecting what is real, what is factual, in favor of a false belief is the ultimate form of denial. In discussing fundamentalist Christianity, Tim Rymel ('Has Evangelical Christianity Become Sociopathic?') put it this way: "It's common for us to avoid cognitive dissonance, when our beliefs dictate one thing, but our experiences show us something else is true. We call this living in denial" "But when we choose our "truth" while coldly watching a fellow human being suffer, we've crossed a line of mental health." 'Sociopath' is a diagnostic category in the Diagnostical and Statistical Manual (DSM) of the American Psychiatric Association, which includes 16 characteristics of the diagnosis for sociopathic behavior.

Rymel cites Psychology Today magazine in listing most of those characteristics, which include untruthfulness, insincerity, lack of remorse or shame, pathologic egocentricity, incapacity for love, and general poverty in major affective reaction, appropriate emotional response. Rymel argues that: "The evangelical Christian message is loud and clear. They care for no one but themselves. Their devotion is to the version of Christianity, which calls for ruthless abandonment of immigrants, women, children, even their own, and anyone else who doesn't fall in line with their message. Social Justice, which is mentioned in Bible verses over two thousand times, has been replaced with hardline political ideology. Principle over people, indifference over involvement, judgement over generosity."

He gives examples of the sociopathic behaviors in quotes from evangelicals like, Franklin Graham, Pastor Roger Jimenez of Verity Baptist Church in Sacramento, James Dobson and others. The author is correct in his assessment. This sociopathology is passed from one generation to the next through indoctrination and mind control. As expressed by John Swomley, in discussing the dangers of Christian fundamentalism, "Mind control, including a strong relationship between fundamentalism and prejudice, discrimination, intolerance, and hate crimes, religious fundamentalists support private school vouchers and home schooling rather than public schools where students are taught to think for themselves." Fear is a dominant characteristic of evangelical indoctrination.

For a country built on the myth and folklore of self-reliance and frontier independence, the idea of a powerful government is inherently threatening. The idea that a powerful government could insert itself into the affairs of it's people is a threat, if only in psychological terms. Any regulatory norms are viewed by the religious right as a direct attack on the manifest destiny of the nation. It is an attack on the divine force that underlies American identity and individualism. The bureaucratic and secular state is seen in terms of religious conflict. Anyone related to the state, especially, if they uphold or advocate the founding fathers call (The Federalist Papers) for a strong central government is not just demonized, but he actually becomes a demon in the eyes of his opponents. He is seen as and believed to be the Antichrist of revelation sent to unravel God's plan for America and the world.

American fundamentalist Christians are willfully ignorant of who the Jesus of the Gospels actually was, as it violates their foundational myth of manifest destiny. Christianity, as imagined through the lens of American manifest destiny, has no relation at all to the teaching of Jesus in the gospels. Fundamentalists claim that Jesus was a teacher of free market capitalism (it is a religion of, by and for wall street) and preached a "prosperity gospel." The "prosperity gospel" movement is a natural extension of the frontier entrepreneurialism inspired by the manifest destiny myth. Like manifest destiny the 'prosperity gospel' has nothing to do with Jesus of the gospels. The portrayal of Jesus by the gospels does not, in any way what so ever, support the idea that Christ was a successful businessman or entrepreneur.

As discussed in "Young Jesus" by Dr. Jean Pierre Isbouts, Jesus is called a "tekton" in Greek, i.e. a carpenter, artisan or craftsman. Jesus worked as a laborer in the Greek City of Sepphoris, near the hamlet of Nazareth. His familiarity with agriculture in his many parables indicates that Jesus also learned farming skills necessary for survival in rural Galilee. There is zero evidence that Jesus was involved in the merchant trade that could have brought him riches and social standing in the economy of his time and homeland. The Jesus of the gospels is an itinerant teacher and healer, moving among working class people, fisherman and the like. In fact, Jesus was deeply suspicious and leery of wealthy merchants and landowners. The rich man who wanted to join Jesus was told that to do so, he must give away all his wealth to the poor. (Matthew: 19; 16-24) Dismayed, the wealthy man chose not to join Jesus's movement and left. This is when Jesus made his famous and clear statement: "It is easier for a camel to go through the eye of a needle than for a rich man to enter the Kingdom of God." This incident clearly reveals Christ's attitude toward personal property. The Jesus of the gospels is most at home with nursing the poor, and his opposition was toward the powerful elites of his time, political, economic and religious. This brought his mission, his revolution, to a horrible end. The very event that was the catalyst for the crucifixion was Jesus going into the heart of the Jewish Temple and overturning the money changers in its midst, as well as releasing the sacrificial animals, that served as the economic foundation for the Jewish priesthood. This attack on the rich and powerful made him a political threat that got him labeled as a seditious revolutionary which was punishable by death.

These events, in no way what so ever, support the idea, by even the most delusional stretch of the imagination, that Jesus was some kind of "self-help guru" teaching people how to be economically successful and become rich, as fundamentalist would have us believe. Christ's life story is not instructive in wealth building or a roll model for it. Jesus remained dirt-poor his whole life. Fundamentalists try to re-imagine Jesus as Adam Smith, despite the fact that the Jesus of the gospels condemned wealth accumulation in his criticism of the rich. The earliest Christian community was a socialist commune. The followers of the Jerusalem Church were required to reject private property and give up all their goods to be shared in common with the community and the poor (Acts; 2; 44-45, Acts 4: 32-35). When Jesus told the rich man to give away all his goods and follow him, he was not making a broad point about greed, he was very specifically presenting an actual and specific requirement to be a member of his movement. No matter how much fundamentalists wish or try, the asceticism and anti-materialism at the heart of Christ's words can never be erased. The poor and pacifist Jesus will never be a poster boy for or fit into the box of capitalism, imperialism and manifest destiny, that fundamentalists fantasize about in their own minds. Christ won over the hearts of the crowds exactly because he did not judge the weak or blame the poor for their plight. He offered love, kindness, healing and forgiveness for all. Fundamentalists are capable only of the most vial hatred and ugliness, especially toward the poor and oppressed. Jesus inspired within people a hunger for something more than the kingdom of this material world. Jesus pointed to the kingdom of God that his followers could find within themselves through humility, service, and compassion. This hunger cannot be satiated with all the glitter and glitz, shiny baubles, bells, whistles and flashing lights offered by the free enterprise system.

American fundamentalists do not appreciate the wondrous beauty they have in the life and character of Jesus Christ, their teacher. They reject Jesus rather than committing to doing the hard work of molding their lives according to his simple but powerful example. They reject the beauty and greatness they have in Christ's living example and instead, give only hypocritical lip service to his life and legacy with distorted, twisted and empty words. Christ's simple actions of kindness, generosity, compassion and love feed the soul incomparably more than the irrational, illogical, bordering on insanity, complex twisted and distorted theology, fundamentalists use to explain and justify, in their own minds, their beliefs and actions. It is Christ's living example, his actions, his teachings, that draw people to faith, and not the irrational, illogical convoluted arguments or absurd efforts used by fundamentalists to disguise economics as spirituality.

Many politicians are fundamentalists with a strong theocratic orientation. Predominant among the religious right are Dominionists. Dominionism is an ideology that rose from American Evangelicalism to activate and stimulate the Christian right, especially politically, and it became the defining feature of modern politics and culture on the right. Dominionism is the theocratic idea that God has called conservative Christians to exercise "dominion" over society, by taking control of political, social and cultural institutions. Dominionists celebrate Christian nationalism which is closely related to white nationalism. They promote religious supremacy, they have no respect for other religions or even other versions of Christianity. Among other things, they endorse theocracy and believe that the Ten Commandments and the biblical law, should replace America's civil law system, even the constitution.

Dominionism became the ideological engine of the Christian right. They see politicians that they elect to office as fulfilling a religious destiny. They see the election of people like Ted Cruz and Donald Trump as the fulfillment of biblical prophecy, that "God would anoint Christian 'kings' to preside over an 'end-time transfer of wealth' from the wicked to the righteous." Statements like this expose the greed of the religious right, when in their mind, in the end-times, all material wealth on earth will become theirs. Political figures like Ted Cruz are believed to be anointed by God to help Christians in their desire to "go to the marketplace, the financial centers, and occupy the land and take dominion over it." It is pure un-adulterated greed. They believe that this 'end-time transfer of wealth' will relieve Christians of all financial woes, allowing true believers to ascent to a position of economic, political, social and cultural power in which they can maintain their position and build a Christian civilization in material comfort.

Cruz and others embrace the theology of seven mountains (7M) dominionism, which calls for the religious right to take utter control of seven leading institutions in society; family, religion, education, media, entertainment, business and government. Cruz and others are also Christian nationalists, and when they speak of things like 'religious liberty', they mean it as a code for defending and promoting the right of Christians to hold social and cultural authority and privilege over all others. They see themselves as engaged in the battle for dominion. There are many dominionist politicians and public officials at all levels of government who shape political discourse.

The 'far religious right' promotes the idea that Christians must not only dominate society, but institute and enforce the old testament biblical law as the law of the land with a literalist interpretation. Theirs is a biblical rationale and theory of government and public policy development. They push conservative fundamentalism into aggressive political engagement. Their notion of bringing forth "dominion-man" is to promote and establish a biblical worldview. They push home schooling, and work to give maximum latitude to private Christian schools in issues, like teaching creationism as science and minimizing accreditation standards. Preachers of the 7M Dominionism teach that there will be a flood of supernatural powers allowing them to defeat and take dominion over nations. These and reconstructionist Christians also believe in a vastly decentralized form of government.

Theirs is an optimistic theology of inevitable victory assured by God's will, thus, political action is called for and necessary. Pre-millennial dispensationalists believe that in the end times, true Christians will be "raptured" into the clouds, and Jesus will return to defeat the forces of Satan. They were, however, not oriented or disposed to political action, certainly not aggressive political action, but that changed with the influence of post-millennialist Christian re-constructionists. They argued that Jesus could not return until the world had become perfectly Christian and the faithful had ruled for 1,000 years. Some advocate for a world war III which would evolve around a war between Christianity and all other religions.

The post millennials required political action in order to build nations based on biblical principles and biblical laws. An additional strain of dominionist thought and political action was to theocratize the Republican Party and emphasize the need for aggressive militant Christian resistance. Randall Terry of Operation Rescue in his 1995 book stated: "I gladly confess that I want to see civil law in America restored to and based on the law given by Moses on Mount Sinai." He considers biblical law and the ten commandments to be the best law possible, it is "flawless, infallible and unimprovable." In 7M theology the term "mountains" is sometimes used interchangeably with "spheres" or "gates".

Wagner in his 2008 book uses the concept "sphere sovereignty," the idea that all areas of life must be brought under a comprehensive biblical worldview. "We have an assignment from God to take dominion and transform society." Religious freedom as established by the founding fathers is seen by dominionists as a weakness that they can use and exploit to advance their movement and agenda. Dominionist leaders recognize Jeffersonian notions of religious freedom and the society they want as entirely mutually exclusive. They use, for example, the doctrine of religious liberty "to gain independence for Christian schools until we train up a generation of people who know that there is no religious neutrality, no neutral law, no neutral education, and no neutral civil government. Then they will get busy in constructing a bible-based social, political and religious order which finally denies the religious liberty of the enemies of God."

They view the Jeffersonian idea of religious equality under the law as tyranny. They want to change the constitution so that only Christians can hold public office. There is no room for religious liberty in a dominionist society. Wagner stated at a NAR conference that "Dominion has to do with authority and subduing, and it relates to society." "Dominion has to do with control, dominion has to do with rulership." "Dominion means ruling as kings." "So, we are kings for dominion." Theocracy is clearly the goal. The strategy to achieve dominion is prolific reproduction and indoctrination of Christian children.

The creation of a Christian army includes adoption and passing laws which allow only Christian parents (a man and a woman) to legally adopt children. Most of their children are home schooled with the explicit goal of Christian education being dominion. The government officials that emerge from their ranks will be informed by a "biblical worldview" and their very purpose must be to establish the kingdom of God on earth. Donald Trump throughout his campaign and presidency has courted the far religious right, who do not believe that "there is any such thing as separation of church and state." ('With God on Our Side: The Rise of the Religious Right in America', William Martin, Also, PBS documentary).

The 'far religious right' is deeply embedded in American politics at all levels. They are among the most prominent politicians in the country and have played major roles in three presidential elections in a row. Donald Trump has and does enjoy and benefit significantly their support. They have declared that they will use Trump to "expose darkness and perversion" and that God is using Trump to achieve His purposes. They argue that God used Cyrus, the Pagan King of Persia (in the biblical book of Isaiah) to free the Jews from their captivity of 70 years in Babylon and to help build the temple in Jerusalem. God used the pagan Cyrus, they argue, as a "wrecking ball" for His purposes and so God is using Trump in the same way. They believe that God is using Trump to challenge "an increasingly hostile anti-Christian culture." ('Christian Reconstruction', Michael J. McVicar).

They have sold their souls and Christianity to Donald Trump, who has partaken freely of practically every vice, depravity and immoral act known to humankind. He is a corrupt, immoral con man and bully. Michael Gerson, a former Bush speechwriter and current columnist, in an essay entitled "The Last Temptation" in the Atlantic, angrily bemoans the loss of evangelical credibility. "The moral convictions of many evangelical leaders have become a function of their partisan identification. This is not mere gullibility, it is utter corruption." Evangelicals are "negative, censorious, and oppositional." Their core base is the Southern Baptist Conference, who defended slavery and then segregation, and today oppose things like women's basic equality as human beings.

Like Trump, evangelicals distrust science, dismiss racial discrimination, believe that immigrants threaten American values, and worry about extremism among American Muslims, whose religion Franklin Graham has raved against as "an evil and wicked religion." Evangelical preacher Rick Warren does

109

not see anything evil in barring women from divorcing abusive violent spouses. He believes women should obey even the most violent and abusive husbands. Racism is also not a disqualifier for office of president for Trump supporters. They are deeply racist, and racism is their bottom line ('An insider explains how rural Christian white America has a dark and terrifying underbelly', Forsetti.; 'Church of Hypocrisy', Katha Pollitt).

Trump has remade America in the image of fundamentalism and himself; angry, hateful, and ugly. The U.S. has been losing influence in several areas, and Trump is accelerating that loss of influence. Trump branded Africa as "shit-hole countries." The U.S. has been losing influence across the continent for years and China's influence is increasing and spreading there. The racist Trump views Africa with general disregard and with disdain. Trump has insulted scores of nations and has projected the worst of American xenophobia, racism, small-mindedness and vulgarity overseas, while undercutting U.S. allies. Trump is making America ugly in a deeply interconnected world. He wants to isolate the U.S. The America Trump projects overseas is an anxious, afraid, violent, hateful and ugly one. It is a mirror image of fundamentalist Christian America.

Fundamentalist Christians overwhelmingly voted for and still support Donald Trump because they strongly believe he will cause the world to end. How is it that evangelicals could support a person who has literally bragged about sexual assaults, who lies perpetually and pathologically. He is a person who admitted that he never asks God for forgiveness and has very little knowledge of the bible. They do not question Trump because they believe that he was chosen by God to be president and to question Trump is to question God. They believe that Trump was ordained by God to usher in the "end times." Fundamentalists believe that a unified Israel with control over Jerusalem will facilitate the construction of a new Jewish temple and set the groundwork for the end of times.

110

The trigger for the start of the end times is Israel's political boundaries being reestablished to what God promised the Israelites, according to the bible. This was written over 2,700 years ago, by no one really knows who, and edited with the political and economic interests from numerous Popes and Kings. Other parts were written by different people in different periods of time. Trump officially recognized Jerusalem as the capital of Israel. By recognizing Jerusalem as the capital of Israel, Trump most likely killed any chance of a negotiated peace in the middle east. The majority of fundamentalists, after two years of Trump's presidency, still fully support Trump today, and the announcement about Jerusalem played a big role in that. Fundamentalists believe in pre-millennialism, the belief that the second coming of Christ will rule over a peaceful and prosperous earth (Newsweek; 1/12/18). Israel is a key part of the story because fundamentalists believe in events that are fundamental to ushering in the end times. Trump's recognizing Jerusalem as the capital of Israel is part of the fulfillment of the biblical prophecy to bring about the second coming of Christ. Fundamentalists also voted for and still support Trump because, among other things, he promised to protect religious liberties and elect anti-abortion supreme court justices. Primary among those promises made to his racist fundamentalist base was to dismantle anything America's first black president accomplished. Fundamentalists take Trump's presidential victory as proof in their own mind that trump's presidency was according to God's will and ordained by God.

The fundamentalist God is an unjust, unforgiving, blood thirsty, sadomasochistic, merciless, vicious, vindictive, vengeful, retributive, punishing God. Hundreds of statements from the scriptures, describe and delineate their God. Here is just a couple: For example: Unjust and Vindictive; "I the Lord your God am a jealous God, punishing children for the inequity of parents, to the third and fourth generation of those who reject me." Deuteronomy; 5: 9. "I will take vengeance, and I will spare no man." Isaiah; 47: 3. The fundamentalist God even advocated and called for cannibalism.

"You shall eat the flesh of your sons, and you shall eat the flesh of your daughters." Leviticus; 26: 28-29. "And I will CAUSE them to eat the flesh of their sons and the flesh of their daughters, and they shall eat everyone the flesh of his friends." Jeremiah; 19: 7-9. ('God the Most Unpleasant Character in All Fiction', Dan Barker).

The Donald Trump administration indeed is a reflection of the hate, meanness and ugliness of the G.O.P., and the 'far religious right.' The Trump administration is an eerie de-ja-vu of the likes of P.T. Barnum, entertainer, purveyor of fiction, fantasy and the fantastic, who once sarcastically declared that: "There is a sucker born every minute." This comment certainly exposes his view and opinion of his fellow humankind. They are to be taken advantage of, ripe fruit for the picking. Donald Trump is also such a creature of fantasy. Driven by resentment of the "establishment," he doesn't like experts or science because they interfere with his desire to believe or pretend that fictions are facts, to feel the truth. Donald Trump sees conspiracies everywhere there is criticism or opposition to him.

Trump exploits the myths of white racial victimhood. His case of failure to grow up, spoiled, impulsive, moody, a seventy plus year old brat is extreme. "He is P.T. Barnum," his sister, a federal judge said to his biographer Tim O'Brian. Trump told O'Brian that he understood that any racket in America could be turned into an entertainment racket. It says something about the character of a person who literally sees everything as a "racket," even our government. Trump must have known what historian Daniel Boorstin saw coming in politics. "Our national politics has become a competition for images or between images, not between ideals," because we live in a "world where fantasy is more real than reality." "Strictly speaking, there is no way to unmask an image. An image, like any other false event, becomes all the more interesting with our every effort to debunk it."

Donald Trump waited to run for president until a critical mass of Americans had decided politics was a show and a sham (in Trump's view, a "racket" like everything else), that a gigantic conspiracy consisting of "the press, the talk-show experts, the campaign strategists, the political parties, even the candidates themselves, has rigged the game." Like P.T. Barnum, Donald Trump panders to American's extreme penchant for magical thinking. "I play to people's fantasies," his ghostwriter, on Trump's behalf, wrote in 'The Art of the Deal.' "People want to believe that something is the biggest and the greatest and the most spectacular." In Trumps view, that overrides any requirements for facts. For him, if you feel something is true, then it is true.

Trump is the ultimate in narcissism. He believes something is true based on nothing but his feelings, not facts. Hannah Arendt escaped Nazi Germany. In 'The Origins of Totalitarianism,' she states: "The essential conviction shared by all ranks" in a totalitarian movement, "from fellow traveler to leaders is that politics is a game of cheating." In essence, government is a "racket." What Arendt wrote next was downright frightening. Donald Trump could have authored it. ('Fantasyland How America Went Haywire A 500-Year History', Kurt Andersen). Trump and his fundamentalist cohorts are literally the antithesis of early Christianity and Christian beliefs.

During the new testament period and beyond, many Christian communities practiced forms of sharing, redistribution and communal living. In the new testament, Jesus in Matthew 25: 31-46, identifies himself with the hungry, the poor, the sick, and the prisoners. Luke 10: 25-37 follows the statement "you shall love your neighbor as yourself" with the question "and who is my neighbor?" Jesus gives the response that the neighbor includes anyone in need, even people we might be expected to shun in the parable of the good Samaritan. Jesus was a socialist, a radical social ethicist. His ideas and teachings influenced many critics of capitalism, including all manner of socialists, both secular and religious. They criticized corporate sweatshops, widening inequality and the imperialism of expanding capitalism, which was causing widespread human and spiritual suffering.

They blamed a ruthless expanding economy, the "God of money," for pervasive violence and the consistent marginalization of more and more people. They considered unfettered capitalism as a tyranny and criticized the idolatry of money. They called for a guarantee that all citizens be assured dignified work with livable wages, education and healthcare. They argued that capitalism is an economy of exclusion and inequality of legalized theft, and it kills. Christians like Francis Bellamy, a Baptist minister and the author of the original Pledge of allegiance, which did not contain the words "under God," who follow Jesus's radical social ethics, the social gospel of Christ, believe capitalism to be idolatrous and rooted in greed and considered it to be an immoral system and even a sin.

Christian socialists identify the cause of social problems like inequality to be the greed generated by capitalism. They rejected an affluent society, characterized by a widening gap between the rich and the rest, rejected the undue and unfair influence of big business and wall street, which threatened freedom and the unabashed greed of the super-rich, all in the presence of widespread and persistent poverty and hunger. Christian socialism has a long tradition. The emergence of modern capitalism in the 1800's drew many critics who based their criticisms of capitalism on Jesus's teachings and life. Jesus said in Matthew 6: 24, "No one can serve two masters." "Either he will hate one and love the other, or he will be devoted to one and despise the other. You cannot serve both God and mammon."

In Luke 12: 15 Jesus warns, "Watch out! Be on your guard against all kinds of greed; a man's life does not consist in the abundance of his possessions." Jesus was also talking about those who rule over others and warned them to be kind to others. Religious leaders thus played a role in the Christian backlash to capitalism, including Pope Leo XIII (1810-1903) as well as Pope Francis in 2013 in 'The Joy of the Gospel.' Pope Leo was concerned about the widespread dehumanizing conditions in which many workers labored. He argued for the workers' rights to form unions and strike. He argued that workers have a moral right to just wages, rest and fair treatment. He called for a more just and fair equal distribution of society's resources and production. Pope Leo asserted under Christian morality, Jesus's "least of mine" have a claim to special consideration. He attacked capitalism for it's endorsement of greed, it's concentration of wealth and its mistreatment of workers.

Francis Bellamy (1855-1931) an American Baptist minister, likewise, championed the right of working people and a more equal distribution of wealth and income, which he argued was according to Jesus's teachings, and he preached against the evils of capitalism. Bellamy consistently described Jesus Christ as a socialist. Bellamy wrote the "pledge of allegiance" in 1892 in protest to gilded age greed, immoral rampant materialism and extreme individualism. Bellamy wrote, "with liberty and justice for all." Bellamy did not include the words "under God" in the original pledge, which were added by Congress in 1953, because he was a very strong believer in Jefferson's separation of church and state.

Many of America's critics of capitalism rooted their views in their Christian faith. Many of them were protestant clergy. Also, among the critics were some of America's most influential thinkers, such as Philosopher John Dewey, the founder of modern education in America along with William James. Others included Kathrine Lee Bates, who wrote "America The Beautiful," Upton Sinclair, Albert Einstein and in recent years Martin Luther King. Jesus condemned income inequality (Luke; 12: 5) as well as unfettered consumerism (Like; 12: 16-21.) This entire passage takes on a rather communistic outlook, especially with the command to sell our possessions and give what we have to charity (Like; 12: 33).

Jesus never spoke to the individual, he always spoke to crowds about his teachings, and he left them to the disciples as a whole. He spoke to Israel as a whole. (Hebrews 1: 1-3) Jesus also addressed government, rulers, and policy, when he takes the whips to the temple animals. The religious authorities had some government sway. One could not speak to the tax collectors without it looking like one was speaking to or about Rome. Individuality is not an ancient concept. Jesus came to save collectively the people of God and the world. Jesus condemns in the parable in Luke 12 any notion that the consumer or consumerism rules. The parable contained in Luke 19: 12-27 praises the person who did not make any money.

Matthew 25: 31-46 focuses on a charitable life as the way to Heaven. Truly in the scriptures, the teachings and life of Jesus Christ, bring forth political statements, such as, "it is better to give than receive," and the language of "kingdom" (John 18: 36) is a political statement, Jesus was super-political. Jesus would have railed at the inhumanity and horrors of modern capitalism. The problem with many Christians is that they don't act like Christ, and they don't want to. They are not true Christians. They worship capitalism and wealth, while only giving lip service to Christianity. They attempt to hide behind Christianity by self-identification and much public proclamation of their faith. They display, advertise and preach their love of Jesus as self-righteous, and saved.

Donald Trump can be described as a by-product of the 'far religious right' ('How Dominionists Gained Control of The Trump Campaign', Jonathan Goodman). The 'far religious right' will always be there. Religious fanaticism will always be a threat to Democracy and freedom. Capitalism will always be a threat. Together, there is no greater threat to Democracy and freedom. The founding fathers told us that the "eternal vigilance" of an "enlightened" citizenry is the very foundation of Democracy and freedom. The author shows no kindness or mercy to those who would destroy America's freedoms', so they can act out their asinine religious fantasies that have no relation at all to Jesus's "Social Gospel."

Donald Trump won four-fifths of the votes of white Evangelical Christians, yet, Trump's background and beliefs could hardly be more incompatible with traditional Christian models of life and leadership. Fundamentalists dismiss Trump's moral scruples, despite the fact that they smack far more of Nietzsche than of Christ. Fundamentalist voters were the decisive factor in Trump's improbable victory, and the Trump administration's outreach to white evangelicals has been utterly consistent. Trump's allied religious leaders have an open door to the white house that constitutes "unprecedented access," as declared buy the president of the Southern Evangelical Seminary.

Pastor David Jeremiah has compared Jared Kushner and Ivanka Trump to Joseph and Mary: "it's just like God to use a young Jewish couple to help Christians." Jerry Falwell Jr. believes that evangelicals have "found their dream president" in Trump. Loyalty to Trump is unquestioned and extends to other political figures. Falwell and Franklin Graham support any candidate supported by Trump and vouch for Trump's "concern for Christian values." The utter corruption of the moral convictions of evangelicals have become a function of their political affiliation and ideology. They engage in intensive political tribalism and hatred for political opponents.

One of their most common activities is out and out hate mongering. Trump, without any doubt what so ever, is the least traditional Christian figure in temperament, behavior, and belief to become president of the United States. The evangelicals who put Trump in office believe that human effort, particularly political, can hasten the arrival of the second coming. They believe that Trump was ordained by God to be president of the United States. As put by evangelical Republican Senator Strange of Alabama: "Trump's presidency is a biblical miracle."

Evangelicalism had its better days. Evangelicalism was the predominant religious tradition in mid-19th century America; it welcomed progress and was hopeful about the future. About 75 years later, it had become a danger to freedom, even though religious progressives sought common ground between Christianity and the new science and higher criticism.

However, fundamentalists and capitalism took their toll. Religious conservatives rebelled against modernism in a series of firings and heresy trials to maintain control of seminaries, to contest progressive ideas. The religiously orthodox published the series of books, called the 'fundamentals,' as a reaction, which engendered the term fundamentalism. Fundamentalism embraced strict traditional religious views which gave zero leeway for questioning or variation to any degree what so ever. It became simplistic and extremely literal in its reading of the scriptures. In reacting against evolution, it became utterly anti-science in orientation. It came to regard any progressive ideas, especially social in nature like "social justice," as dangerous liberal ideas or evil.

All progressive social concerns whether political or private, became dangerous ideas, if not evil, and the work of Satan among evangelicals. Wealthy libertarians and wall street seized the opportunity to put a yoke around Jesus's neck and harness him to serve their interests. They did this by becoming allies with the 'far religious right.' For example, Fox News and conservative talk radio targeted these groups and soon became a vastly great influence on evangelical's political identity. Fox News and conservative radio talk shows cemented the alliance by blending into one, libertarian, capitalist economics and politics with fundamentalism. Politics, economics and religion became largely no longer distinguishable one from another.

The primary fundamentalist political narrative is adversarial, angry, mostly imaginary, tales about the persecutions of fundamentalism by it's cultural enemies. Fundamentalists comprise the single largest religious demographic in the U.S. and make up half the republican political coalition. They are well-funded by rich libertarian, conservative would-be oligarchs, like the DeVos family who have contributed hundreds of millions of dollars to their cause. The attitude of the fundamentalist movement was eagerly exploited by the G.O.P. Fundamentalists, who were alienated, were happily and effectively courted to join for example, the Reagan coalition, a solid base from which to promote "trickle down" or "supply side" economics. It is a scheme devised to shift massive amounts of wealth, through the tax system, from the bottom and middle, to the few at the top.

Fundamentalist ethics and morality, especially in terms of social relations and engagement, are out and out primitive and barbaric. Fundamentalists get their theory of social relations from a legalistic and literal interpretation of the bible. The Christian bible offers for, example, approving accounts of genocide and recommends the stoning to death of insubordinate children. The scriptures even endorse cannibalism. Theirs is a stone age ethics. Fundamentalists maintain their ideology and theories of social relations by following the direction of the political movement that is defending and exploiting them, which are the interests of oligarchs, the G.O.P. and their rich funders.

Fundamentalist political engagement is morbidly negative, censorious, oppositional and obsessed with sex, among other things. They consistently vote for politicians that wage war on and crucify those who Jesus referred to as "The least of mine." The ethnic and racial insularity of most white fundamentalists contributes to their extreme racism and bigotry. Evangelical churches largely are segregated on Sunday. Nearly all denominations with large numbers of evangelicals are much less racially diverse than the country overall. Donald Trump rode the wave of anger and frustration into the white house, a wave that rural evangelical Americans were experiencing. They were anxious and scared, and he played them like a fool.

Some rural Americans were afraid and ignorant. Theydon't understand the causes of their own problems. They haven't got a clue as to the sources of their own fears. Ironically, they have no interest in understanding or even finding out. They don't want to know why they feel the way they do or why they are struggling. They do not want in any way to look at or question their own behavior, beliefs, and decisions. Their religion conditions them to not think, let alone question. They want only to listen to easy answers, spoon fed to them with ready made scapegoats for their situation. This self-imposed, self-righteous ignorance prevents them from understanding their problems, themselves, or the reasons for their fear, anger and frustrations. They do not want to admit that they are first and foremost racists and capitalists, with all the baggage that comes with them. They are their own worst enemy.

For the 'far religious right,' Lilly-white Christian Jesus with blue eyes and blond hair, literally and figuratively is king. This belief is firm, in spite of the fact that the great weight of objective evidence points to a dark-skinned Jesus and 12 dark-skinned disciples. Science has established that Jesus most likely looked more like Yasser Arafat than anyone. The oldest known image of Jesus and the disciples depicts Jesus as black, which is in the Coptic museum in Cairo, Egypt. The new testament states many times the revolutionary Jesus slipped away into the crowds, and the religious officials or other authorities, when looking for him, frequently could not find him. Jesus looked like any other rabbi of the day, and he wasn't in the U.S.A.

There are dozens of accounts where Jesus, the revolutionary, simply slipped away and blended into the crowds, for example, John 5: 13, 7: 11, 11: 56 and Luke 4: 30. The fundamentalist belief system is a closed system. It is neither open nor conducive to even second thoughts, let alone open for questioning, introspection, learning and certainly not change. Fundamentalism is not open to outside criticism. Rural white Christian America will never listen to anything not imbedded in or supported by their belief system, and they will not listen to anyone outside the tribe. They are as tribal as the most primitive aborigines. They do not understand themselves or the world they live in because of this. Instead, they fabricate a fantasyland in their own minds which they take literally as reality. To them information of any kind or any proof, regardless how concrete, cannot be true if it contradicts in any way, in any amount, their insanely entrenched beliefs. They believe that science, facts, knowledge, education are not to be trusted or believed, because they are the enemy of fundamentalism and are fostered by Satan, because fundamentalism itself is not built on facts. Fundamentalism is a producer of self-righteous racism. Fundamentalists believe they are made in God's image; therefore, they are superior to non-whites and everyone else is an imperfect flawed and cursed copy. Non-whites are the color they are because of their sins, original or otherwise. Blacks have dark skin because they were rejected by God; they are cursed. God cursed and rejected them for a reason. Since God cursed them, treating them as equals would be denying God's will. Besides, why would you waste your time on someone who is destined for hell?

Fundamentalists carry the bible and proclaim that "everyone is a child of God" even though for them, and their 'whiteness', some of God's children are more favored or saved than others, and skin color is the dividing line between those who are most favored or saved and those who are not. Fundamentalists are as closed minded as a rock. They are literally unreachable with facts. They are not open to thought, let alone argument. To even try to argue is useless, because you are arguing against God. Many rural fundamentalist, white Americans are neither open to nor listen to educated arguments based on objective facts, if they go against their fundamental belief system.

Fundamentalism is a belief system literally devoid of logic and rational thought processes. Internal change, even microscopic change (that's an instrument of science) occurs very rarely, and if it does, it always lags far behind reality. They are not familiar with or used to change. Like any primitive tribe, they confront it in fear and horror. Even the notion of change itself is evil, a temptation of Satan. Most rural white, fundamentalist Christian Americans who are the base support of Trump are anti-intellectual, anti-science, anti-fact bigoted racists, and identify with or relate to only those who are just like them. They listen to people like Sean Hannity and Bill O'Reilly, as well as any fundamentalist preachers who sell themselves as being just like them, tells them what they want to hear, that is, what they already believe (mainly the superiority of white Christian America.)

For fundamentalists anyone who is not just like them and does not think just like them, with the same world view, is a threat and evil. They have no connection, no relation to facts or reality, nor do they matter one iota. They choose to fabricate in their own mind a fantasyland of make believe, an alternative reality and they want to impose it on everyone else. It is in this sense, that fundamentalists are arguably, not sane. Their fears will never be alleviated or go away because their fears are not rational or justified. Their fears are generated by lies and falsehoods in their own minds and exist in a closed-off fundamentalist belief system and worldview. When a centuries old book written by pre-scientific, uneducated writers, who believed among other things that the earth was flat, was subject to translation many times by special interests and was given the ultimate authority, the ultimate reality, the ultimate truth, then nothing will save these believers from their own self-imposed insanity and hell.

A fundamentalist cannot even entertain, even conceptualize the possibility he might be wrong. If a preacher says it is so, then it is so, no questions asked or even entertained. The emotional and psychological need to be right outweighs all else. That need is based on insecurity, ignorance and primitive fear. Fundamentalists, incapable of questioning themselves, engage in a lot of irrational, fact-exempt scapegoating. It is much less threatening and more emotionally secure to look to scapegoats rather than evaluate your own beliefs. Scapegoating is prominent among Christian fundamentalists who "know" they are superior because of things like the color of their skin or the religion they claim to follow. They 'know' they cannot be wrong because they were born in the "image" of an infallible, inerrant God. Thus, in their own mind, any and all problems they experience is because of someone else.

That rural white fundamentalist/evangelical/born again Christian Americans are racist and bigoted is not new because the country was built on racism and bigotry. It was built on greed and barbarism. White America is the reason racism and bigotry still exist, and fundamentalism is its strongest base. There are honest truths that rural Christian white Americans don't want to admit, let alone accept, because they would have to admit that they are their own worst enemy. One such truth is that their economic situation is largely, if not wholly, the result of voting over and over for "trickle down" or "supply side" economics, that by its very design is and has been the largest redistribution of wealth from the bottom and middle to the top in the history of the United States. Against their own best interests, fundamentalists consistently vote over and over again for things like "trickle down" economics. To explain this to them would be like trying to explain quantum physics to a squirrel.

In fact, practically every single malady against which fundamentalists complain is either a falsehood or created by their own behavior and belief system. The real problem is a total lack of understanding by most rural fundamentalist, Christian white Americans of why they believe, vote and behave the way they do. Their Christian beliefs and morals are only extended to fellow white Christians, and their belief systems are constructed against progress, which is why they do not experience it. Rural Christian white Americans are embedded and trapped in fundamentalist belief systems and worldview. They don't trust anyone outside their tribe.

123

They have been fed a regular and consistent diet of misinformation and lies for generations. They feel left out and behind by a world they don't understand and don't really care to. They are un-willing to understand their own problems and deeply believe that they are superior to all races. Their superiority does not reflect their experiences in life and that is frustrating. Their cognitive dissonance is immense because their fears are based on myths and lies. They vote against their own best interest as long as it hurts minorities more than them. They, not minorities are their own worst enemy.

The fundamental voice is apocalyptic to say the least. Franklin Graham has declared that the country "has taken a nosedive off of the moral diving board into the cesspool of humanity." Their rhetoric is an insanely pessimistic depiction of our not perfect, but wonderful country. Politics in a Democracy is essentially anti-apocalyptic, based on the idea that an "enlightened" "eternally vigilant" and active citizenry is capable of improving its lot. Evolution is progressive, and it is the main point of the Evangelical's rejection and contention with modernity. Evolution is a scientific fact. It is objectively true based on irrefutable and overwhelming evidence. Human dignity is not served by obscuring and fantasizing human origins. Fundamentalists deny this and insist that Christian faith must reject reason. It is practically the rejection of sanity.

Fundamentalists are Trump's army of enablers and remain the most loyal element of the Trump coalition. They are very eager to act as his biblical shield and sword to smite his enemies. Fundamentalists/Evangelicals are highly vulnerable to a message of rhetoric of resentful, pessimistic, declinist populism and apocalyptic warnings, which is one thing that Donald Trump gave them. For example, "Our country is going to hell" or "We haven't seen anything like this, the carnage all over the world." Trump was adopting premillennialism to populism. When he spoke about America in decline and headed toward destruction, which could be stopped only by recovering and reinstituting the certainties of the past, he was strumming the strings of fundamentalist belief. Thus, he held out the promise to "Make America great again."

Trump is not just a propagandist but a manipulator of madness. Trump told a Liberty University Audience: Christianity is "under siege." "Relish the opportunity to be an outsider." "Embrace the label." And, protecting Christianity, Trump argues is a job for a bully. Fundamentalists view themselves as an oppressed minority that requires a strongman to rescue it. Trump pushed this view, and it got him elected. One reason is that fundamentalists are very authoritarian in worldview. A prominent group of fundamentalists leaders Dobson, Graham and Falwell among them argue that all of Trump's flaws are worth the more favorable treatment of Christians by the government. They have castigated his critics on every point. It is amazing to hear religious leaders defend profanity, ridicule and cruelty as hallmarks of authenticity and dismiss decency as a dead language.

These religious leaders are providing religious cover for Trump. They are putting aside Christianity itself for moral squalor. They endorse bullying, undermine public integrity, spread cynicism about Democracy and foster the unraveling of social cohesion and restraints. These fundamentalist leaders have ceased to be moral leaders in any meaningful sense. They wallow in moral squalor. They are un-American and anti-freedom. They are would-be petty and self-righteous dictators. Trump is a racist. His father was once arrested in New York for participating in a KKK riot. Indeed, Trump's political allies, his defense of Nazi's white supremacists and white nationalists are part of his appeal. Fundamentalist leaders have associated the Christian faith with racism, nativism, misogyny and mocking the disabled.

Fundamentalist leaders are not only eager to act as Trump's cover, shield and sword but see it as their religious duty to protect and defend him. Their mission is to be his army of enablers.

Fundamentalists have no decency left, no interest in it at all. Democracy's values of empathy, honesty, integrity, self-restraint and caring for others is a moral structure. In contrast, fundamentalists legitimize cruelty, corruption, prejudice, falsehood and hatred. Fundamentalists have brought the Christianity of the middle ages to 21st century America. Christianity is anything but love thy neighbor when Christians become a political interest group scrambling for power, benefits and yes even mammon, riches and wealth, at the expense of others and their country.

They reject the welfare of others and the whole. They give a whole new meaning to the "me generation." They are eons away from 1st century Christians and the teachings of Jesus Christ. They are not Christians in any sense of the term. Jesus's dream went awry in the hands of Christians influenced by capitalism and greed, self-centeredness and selfishness, idiocy and ignorance. From the time of the first pilgrims to America, the stage was set against Jesus's dream. It was a stage characterized by problems of geography, demographics, religious diversity and conflicts. Starting in the early 20th century fundamentalists, evangelicals, and born-again Christians sealed its doom and put Jesus back in the tomb.

Resources considered secondary references or background in the writing of this book are not included.

References

Abanes, Richard, *'American Militias: Rebellion, Racism and Religion'*, Intervarsity Press, London, 1996.

Alinsky, Saul, *'Rules for Radicals'*, Random House, N.Y., 1989.

Andersen, Kurt, *'Fantasyland How America Went Haywire A 500-Year History'*, Random House, N.Y., 2017.

Arendt, Hannah, *'The Origins of Totalitarianism'*, Schocken Books, N.Y., 1973.

Armstrong, Karen, *'The Battle for God'*, Alfred A. Knopf, N.Y., 2000.

Ashtari, Shadee, *'KKK Leader Disputes Hate Group Label; We're A ChristianOrganization'*,www.huffingtonpost.com/2014/03/21/virginia-kkk-fliers_n_5008647.html. 2015.

Atran, Scott, *'Talking to the Enemy: Violent Extremism, Sacred Values, and What It Means to be Human'*, Penquin, N.Y., 2011.
.... *'In Gods We Trust: The Evolutionary Landscape of Religion'*, Oxford University Press, Oxford, N.Y., 2002.

Bailyn, Bernard, *'The Barbarous Years'*, Vintage Books, N.Y., 2013.

Barber, William, in foreword to: *'Reconstruction of the Gospel; Finding Freedom From Slaveholder Religion'*, Johnathan Wilson, Hartgrove Mission Audio, 2018.

Barker, Dan, *'God the Most Unpleasant Character in All Fiction'*, Sterling, N.Y., 2016.

Bawer, Bruce, *'Stealing Jesus: How Fundamentalism Betrays Christianity'*, Three Rivers Press, N.Y., 1997.

Becker, Earnest, *'The Denial of Death'*, Simon & Schuster, N.Y., 1973.

Belew, Kathleen, **'Bring the War Home: The White Power Movement and Paramilitary America'**, Harvard University Press, 2018.

Bhangu, Mike, *'War and Religion'*, BBP, B.C., Canada, 2016.

Blaker, Kimberly, *'The Fundamentals of Extremism: The Christian Right in America'*, Green Grove Press, Michigan, 2003.

Blow, Charles M., *'Moore, Trump and the Right's New Religion'*, New York Times, November 16, 2017.

Blumer, Herbert, *'Symbolic Interactionism'*, University of California Press, 1986.

Boorstin, Daniel, *'The Image: A Guide to Pseudo-Events in America'*, Vintage Books, N.Y., 1961.

Borg, Marcus, (ed), *'The Lost Gospel Q, The Original Sayings of J Jesus'*, Ulysses Press, Seastone, 1999.

Brown, DeNeen L., *'The Preacher Who Used Christianity to Revive theKuKluxKlan'*, www.washingtonpost.com/news /retropolis/ wp/2018/04/08/the-preacher-who-used-christianity-to-revive-the-ku-klux-klan.

Clarkson, Frederick, *'Dominionism Rising: A Theocratic Movement Hiding in Plain Sight'*, Public Eye Magazine, Summer, 2016. Also, www.politicalresearch.org.

Cozzolino, Philip J., et. al., *'Self-Related Consequences of Death Fear and Death Denial'*, *Death Studies,* Vol. 38, No. 6, Taylor and Francis Online, 2014.

Crossan, John, *'The Historical Jesus, The Life of a Mediterranean Jewish Peasant'*, Harper Collins, N.Y., 1992.

Delany, Tim, *'Social Deviance'*, Rowman & Littlefield, N.Y., 2017.

Dewey, John, *'Experience and Education'*, Touchstone, N.Y. 1997.
.... *Democracy and Education'*, MacMillan, N.Y., 1916.

Dobson, James and Gary L. Bauer, *'Children at Risk'*, W Publishing Group, Nashville, 1992. (earlier edition unavailable).

Donner, Colonel V., *'The Samaritan Strategy'*, Wolgemuth & Hyatt Pub., Colorado, 1988.

Drummond, Henry, *'The City Without a Church'*, Wilder Publications, Radford, VA., 2008.
.... *'The Greatest Thing in the World'*, Barbour and Company, Ohio, 1990.

Durkheim, Emile, *'The Elementary Forms of Religious Life'*, Trans: Karen Fields, Free Press, N.Y., 1995.
.... *'On Totemism'*, History of Sociology, 5, 2; 79-121, Trans. of 1902 a (i), 1985.
.... *'The Problem of religion and the Duality of Human Nature', in Knowledge and Society; Studies in the Sociology of Culture, Past and Present, JAI Press, 1984.*

Emerson, Michael O. and Christian Smith, *'Divided by Faith; Evangelical Religion and the Problem of Race in America'*, Oxford University Press, N.Y., 2000.

Fisher,Michael,'*TheKuKluxKlan*',http://home.wlu.edu/ lubiut / touchstone/kkk-fisher.htm8/13/2017.

Foreman, Dale, *'Crucify Him: A Lawyer Looks at the Trial of Jesus'*, Zondervan, Grand Rapids, 1990.

Foresetti's Justice, *'An Insider Explains How Rural Christian White America has a Dark and Terrifying Underbelly'*, https://www.rawstory.com/2018/02/insider-explains-rural-christian-white-america-dark-terrifying-underbelly/.

Fosdick, Harry Emerson, *'The Man from Nazareth'*, Pocket Books, N.Y., 1953.
.... *'The Man from Nazareth as his Contemporaries Saw Him'*, Harper & Row, N.Y., 1949.

Frankfort, Henri, *'Chapter VII: Mesopotamia; The Good Life: Before Philosophy*; *The Intellectual Adventure of Ancient Man, an Essay on Speculative Thought in the Ancient Near East.'*, Penquin, N.Y., 1974.

Franklin, Michael and Marian Hetherly, *'How Fundamentalism Affects Society'*, The Humanist, Inquiry Press, N.Y., 1997.

George, Andrew, (trans), *'The Epic of Gilgamesh: The Babylonian Epic Poem and other Texts in Akkadian and Sumerian'*, Penquin, London, 1999.

Gerson, Michael, *'The Last Temptation'*, The Atlantic, April, 2018, www.theatlantic.com/magazine/archieve/2018/04/the-last-temptation/554066/.

Gilens, Martin and Benjamin Page, *'Testing Theories of American Politics; Elites, Interest Groups, and Average Citizens'*, Perspectives on Politics, Fall, 2014.

Gold, Howard J. and Gina E. Russell, *'The Rising Influence of Evangelicalism in American Political Behavior, 1980-2004'*, The Social Science Journal, 44: 3; 554-562, 2007.

Goodman, Jonathan, *'How Dominionists Gained Control Of The Trump Campaign'* http://www.huffingtonpost.com/ entry/ dominionistsgaincontroloftrumpcampaign_us_57c817d0e4b-06c750dd8d25a.

Gorringe, Timothy and Rose Beckham, *'Transition Movements for Churches'*, Canterbury Press, Norwich, 2013.

Greenberg, et.al., *'Evidence for Terror Management Theory II: The Effects of Mortality Salience on Reactions to Those Who Threaten or Bolster the Cultural Worldview'*, Journal of Personality and Social Psychology, 58; (2), 1990.
.... , *'Terror Management Theory of Self-esteem and Cultural World Views: Empirical Assessments and Conceptual Refinements'*, Advances in Experimental Social Psychology, 29: (S61), 1997.

Greenspan, Allen, *'The Age of Turbulence: Adventures in a New World'*, Penguin, N.Y., 2008.

Hamilton, Mark W., *'How Some Evangelical Christians are Complicit in the Cruelty of Politics'*, Dallas Morning News, 3/18/2017.

Hanna, Judith Lynne, *'Naked Truth: Strip Clubs, Democracy, and a Christian Right'*, University of Texas Press, Austin, 2012.

Hedges, Chris, *'American Fascists: The Christian Right and the War on America'*, Free Press, N.Y., 2008.

Heidegger, Martin, *'Being and Time'*, Macquarrie, J., and E. Robinson, (trans), Harper & Row, N.Y., 1963.
.... *'What is a Thing'*, Barton, W.B., and V. Deutsch, (trans), H. Regnery Co., Washington, D.C., 1967.
.... *'The Concept of Time'*, William McNeill (trans) Blackwell, Oxford, 1992.

Hudson, Jackie J., *'Characteristics of the Incestuous Family'*, in: Cathrine Clark Kroeger and James A. Beck (eds), *'Women, Abuse, and the Bible: How Scripture Can Be Used to Hurt or Heal'*, Baker, Grand Rapids, 1996.

Hyman, Irwin, in: *'Spanking on the Decline in U.S. Schools'*, U.S.A. Today, December 2, 1996.

Isbouts, Jean Pierre, *'Young Jesus: Restoring the "Lost Years" of a Social Activist and Religious Dissident'*, Sterling, N.Y., 2008.

Jong, Jonathan, and Jamin Halberstadt, *'Death Anxiety and Religious Belief: An Existential Psychology of Religion'*, Bloomsburg, London, 2016.

Juergensmeyer, Mark, *'Terror in the Mind of God: The Global Rise in Religious Violence'*, University of California Press, 2003.

Kierkegaard, Soren, *'The Sickness Unto Death'*, Wiseblood Classics of Philosophy, 2013.
.... And **Walter Lowrie**, *'Fear and Trembling and the Sickness Unto Death'*, Penguin, N.Y., 2013.

King, Martin Luther Jr., James Washington, (ed), *'A Testament of Hope: The Essential Writings and Speeches of Martin Luther King Jr.*, Harper One, N.Y., 2003.

Krahe, Barbara, *'The Social Psychology of Aggression'*, Psychology Press, N.Y., 2003.

Kroeger, Cathrine Clark and Nancy Nason-Clark (eds), *'Beyond Abuse in the Christian Home: Raising Voices for Change'*, Wipf & Stock, Eugene, Oregon, 2008.

Kruse, Kevin, *'One Nation Under God'*, Basic Books, N.Y., 2015.

Lewis, Andrew R., *'The Rights Turn in Conservative Christian Politics: How Abortion Transformed the Culture Wars'*, Cambridge University Press, 2017.

Linn, Jan G., *'What's Wrong with the Christian Right'*, Brown Walker Press, Boca Raton, Florida, 2004.

Mack, Burton, *'Who Wrote the New Testament'*, Harper Collins, N.Y., 1995.

MacLean, Nancy, *'Behind the Mask of Chivalry'*, Oxford University Press, Oxford, 1995.
.... *'Democracy in Chains'*, Viking, N.Y., 2017.

McVicar, Michael J., *'Christian Reconstruction'*, University of North Carolina Press, 2015.

Martin, William, *'With God on Our Side: The Rise of the Religious Right in America'*, (anglaise) Broche-Juillet, 1997.

Marx, Karl, *'Economic and Philosophic Manuscripts of 1844'*,

Mattil, James F., *'What in the Name of God? Religious Extremism, Fear and Terrorism'*, Global Focus.Org., 2011.

Mayer, Jane, *'Dark Money'*, Doubleday, N.Y., 2016.

Maza, Christina, *'Trump Will Start the End of the World: Claim Evangelicals Who Support Him'*, Newsweek, 1/12/2018.

Meroz, Christianne, *'Jesus of Nazareth Always on the Move'*, Dennis Wierk (trans), Wipf & Stock, Eugene, Oregon, 2017.

Merton, Thomas and William Shannon, *'The Inner Experience: Notes on Contemplation'*, Harper, San Francisco, 2004.

Meyers, Robin, *'Why the Christian Right is Wrong: A Minister's Manifesto for Taking Back Your Faith, Your Flag, Your Future'*, Jossey-Bass, San Francisco, 2006.

Michaux, Henri, *'Stroke by Stroke'*, Archipelago, Brooklyn, 2006.
.... And **Richard Sieburth**, *'A certain Plume'*, Penguin, N.Y. 2018.

Moorjani, Anita, *'What if this is Heaven'*, Hayhouse, Carlsbad, California, 2016.

Needleman, Jacob, *'Money and the Meaning of Life'*, Doubleday, N.Y., 1994.

Newton, Michael, *'The Ku Klux Klan: An Encyclopedia'*, Garland Science, Routledge, Taylor And Francis, 1990.

Oldroyd, Richard, *'Child Sexual Abuse: statistics, Trends, and Case Outcomes'*, http://www2.state.id.us/ag/newrel /2018/ nr_jan232008.htm.

Olson, Laura R. and Adam L. Warber, *'Belonging, Behaving, and Believing: Assessing the Role of Religion on Presidential Approval'*, Political Research Quarterly, 61: 2; 192-204, 2008.

Pickering, W.S.F., (ed), *'Durkheim on Religion: A Selection of Readings with Bibliographies'*, Routledge & Kegan Paul, London and Boston, 1975.

Pinker, Steven, *'Enlightenment Now'*, Viking, N.Y., 2018.

Pollitt, Katha, *'Why Evangelicals---Still! ---Support Trump'*, The Nation, March 22, 2018.
.... *'Church of Hypocrisy'*, The Nation, April 16, 2018.

Rogers, Will, *'The Wit and Wisdom of Will Rogers: An A to Z Compendium of Quotes from America's Best Loved Humorist'*, Alex Ayers (ed), Plume First Trade, Penguin, N.Y., 1995.
.... *'Will Rogers Says .... Favorite Quotations'*, Dr. Reba Collins (ed), Will Rogers Memorial Staff (ed), Neighbors and Quaid, Oklahoma City, 1993.

Rohr, Richard and Mike Morell, *'Meditations: 'Essential Teachings on Love', 'Jesus Plan for A New World: The Sermon on the Mount', 'The Church is Supposed to be an Alternate Lifestyle'*, 2017, Center for Action and contemplation, Daily Meditations, Albuquerque, N.M., 2018.

Rowatt, Wade C., et.al., *'Associations Among Religiousness, Social Attitudes, and Prejudice in a National Random Sample of American Adults'*, Psychology of Religion and Spirituality, 1:1: 14-24, 2009.

Rymal, Tim, *'Has Evangelical Christianity Become Sociopathic'*, www.huffingtonpost.com/entry/has-evangelical-christianity-become-sociopathic-_us_5914ce6fe4b02d6199b2ed92.

Rymer, Russ, *'Genie: A Scientific Tragedy'*, 2cd Ed., Harper Perennial, N.Y., 1994.

Sanders, N.K., *'The Epic of Gilgamesh'*, Penguin Epics, Penguin Classics, Penguin, London, 2006.

Schweitzer, Albert, *'The Quest of Historical Jesus'*, Dover Publications, N.Y., 2005.

Smith, Morton, *'Jesus the Magician: A Renowned Historian Reveals How Jesus Was Viewed by People of His Time'*, Hampton Roads Press, Massachusetts, 2014.
.... *'The Secret Gospel, the Discovery and Interpretation of the Secret Gospel According to Mark'*, The Dawn House Press, Middletown, California, 2005.

Solomon, Sheldon, et.al., *The Worm at the Core: On the Role of Death and Life'*, Random House, N.Y., 2015.

Spong, John Selby, *'Rescuing the Bible from Fundamentalism'*, Harper Collins, N.Y., 1992.

Steele, Tom, *'First Baptist Dallas Pastor Robert Jeffries: Evangelicals Don't Care if Trump Had Sex with Porn Star'*, The Dallas Morning News, March 13, 2018.

Stewart, Kathrine, *'The Good News Club: The Christian Rights Stealth Assault on America's Children'*, Public Affairs, N.Y., 2012.

Struick, Dirk J., (ed), International Publishers, N.Y., 1964.
.... *'Capital: A Critique of Political Economy'*, Samual Moore (trans), Modern Library, Random House, N.Y., 1906.

Swomly, John M., *'Religious Liberty and the Secular State'*, Prometheus Books, N.Y., 1987.

Tawney, R.H., *'Religion and the Rise of Capitalism'*, Routledge, N.Y., 2017.
Terry, Randal A., (Founder) *'Operation Rescue'*, Wichita, Kansas, 1988.

The Dali Lama, *'Beyond Religion Ethics for a Whole World'*, Mariner Books, Boston, 2012.

Thoreau, Henry David, *'Walden'*, Empire Books, CreateSpace Ind. Pub., Amazon, 2018.

Thrower, James, *'The Alternative Tradition: A Study of Unbelief in the Ancient World'*, Mouton Publishers, The Hague, The Netherlands, 1980.

Turner, Jonathan H. and Jan E. Stets, *'The Sociology of Emotions'*, Cambridge University Press, N.Y., 2005.

Weber, Max, *'The Protestant Ethic and the Spirit of Capitalism'*, Merchant Books, N.Y. 2013.
.... and **Talcott Parsons**, *'The Protestant Work Ethic and the Spirit of Capitalism'*, Vigeo Press, N.Y., 2017.

Williams, Daniel K., *'God's Own Party: The Making of the Christian Right'*, (reprint ed)., Oxford University Press, 2012.

Wagnor, C. Peter, *'Dominionism!: How Kingdom Action Can Change The World'*, Chosen, Ada, MI., 2008.

Wong, Paul T.P., and Adrian Tomer, *'Beyond Terror and Denial: The Positive Psychology of Death Acceptance'*, Death Studies, Vol. 35, No 2, Taylor and Francis Online, 2011.

Wyn, Craig Wade, *'The Fiery Cross: The Ku Klux Klan in America'*, Oxford University Press, 1998.

Autographed copies of 'Fear, Religion, Politics; Well I'll Be Darn' may be obtained directly from the author by mailing a check or money order for $16.95 to Dr. John Karlin at P.O. Box 270181, OKC, OK. 73137.
(author will cover taxes and shipping)

For Autographed copies please include:
    1). The name of the person you want it autographed to.
    2). The address to send the book to.

Please allow 10 to 14 days for delivery.

Dr. John Karlin author, professor, researcher, is available for speaking engagements.

For speaking engagements, Dr. Karlin may be contacted at P.O. Box 270181, OKC, OK. 73137
or email at:
karlinfirstnamejohn@yahoo.com

www.ingramcontent.com/pod-product-compliance
Lightning Source LLC
Chambersburg PA
CBHW070805290326
41931CB00011BA/2135